MIND THIEVES

Tom Kenyon

Published by Orb
P.O. Box 98, Orcas, WA 98280
Phone: 360/376-5781
Website: *www.tomkenyon.com*
Email: *office@tomkenyon.com*

ISBN: 1-931032-00-9
Library of Congress Catalog Card Number: 2001088180

Cover Concept: Tom Kenyon
Cube Art: Oceana Eagan
Photo Project Director: Laura Eagan
Book Design/Production: Rebecca A. Cook

A special thanks to Judi Pope Koteen,
for her many hours of help and encouragement.

DEDICATION

This book is dedicated

To the explorers of consciousness,

Who have lived in every culture.

Your footprints are a comfort in the Great Mystery.

And to you, the modern Argonauts of Mind,

Still seeking to find the Philosopher's Stone,

May you find it in this time of darkest human darkness.

Mankind,

Though largely unaware,

Owes you greatest gratitude.

For we are all uplifted by those who live The Path,

From the darkness of ignorance

Into the light of awareness.

NOTICE OF WARNING
TO THE READER

Be forewarned that reading this book may cause a paradigm shift in how you view reality or, in other words, an evolutionary leap in consciousness.

The author and publisher of this manuscript do not accept any responsibility for what might happen to you if you experience such an evolutionary leap in consciousness.

ON THE INDENTATION IN THIS MANUSCRIPT

You will notice throughout this book that the indentation of all paragraphs (with the exception of dialogue) is to the far right side rather than on the left side as is customary in English speaking cultures.

There is a reason for this. One of the goals of this fantasy, besides entertaining and intriguing you, is to shift how you view reality. "Reality" is, I believe, far more vast and mysterious than our minds are capable of conceiving; nevertheless, it is a part of our common nature to "define" reality for ourselves. This definition or boundary of what we deem possible allows us to navigate our way through the world, but at the same time it imprisons the vastness of reality that lies outside our conception of it.

Paradigm shifting allows us to glimpse a broader view of reality, and if we incorporate the shift into our thinking, we can navigate through the world in new ways. This gives us the possibility of discovering new worlds and new ways of perceiving ourselves and others. I believe we are, as a culture, collectively going through such a process.

The odd indentation throughout this book is a gesture if you will, a suggestion to view things in new ways. In many other cultures, especially those in Asia, texts are customarily read from right to left, rather than left to right. By requiring you, the reader, to start each paragraph in an uncommon manner, I am hinting to your subconscious mind that you are embarking on an unusual voyage, one that does not use the same markers or landmarks you are accustomed to.

As you embark on this voyage of discovery, may you find new worlds within yourself. And may we all be enriched by your discoveries.

PRAYER FRAGMENT

Found at Ecstasis in
the Northern New Mexico Desert

In the beginning was the Mystery,
And the Mystery folded itself
Into the containment
Of time and space,
Birthing myriad worlds,
Worlds within worlds,
Multitudinous forms,
Innumerable lives.

May all beings,
Regardless of their station,
Find the comfort of knowing,
The bliss of remembering,
And the ecstasy of reunion.

INTRODUCTION

As a counselor in the fields of transpersonal psychology and hypnosis for over 18 years, I have seen remarkable things occur with my clients when they enter the mysterious worlds of altered perception.

The energy of consciousness and the purpose of awareness are recurring themes in the lives of the persons I attempt to help through the web of personal transformation. This story is drawn from the archetypal dramas of many clients, friends, lovers, and of course, my own *self*. But in order to better explain this enigmatic world of energies, entities, aberrations, and miracles, I must digress into a brief history of modern science, for it is through the eyes of science that our culture views reality and gives it credence or deems it nonsense.

In the old Newtonian view of the world, everything was predictable, from billiard balls and rockets to human psychology. But as we entered the twentieth century and a more volatile period of human history, we discovered, much to the chagrin of classical physicists, that some things are relative. Time and space are not absolutes, much less human psychology.

To further complicate things, within years of Einstein's theory of relativity, physicists uncovered a weird "twilight zone" of the subatomic realm where the law of uncertainty reigned supreme. Suddenly the very underpinnings of our everyday world seemed to be the result of a random-particle madness (or genius, depending upon how you look at it).

The rug was pulled out from under us. And among the casualties, the treasured ideal of an objective observer, hallowed for centuries as the benchmark of hard science, began to tremble under the weight of quantum mechanics.

Bell's Theorem, derived from the observation of atomic particles, basically states that (at the subatomic level, at least) the observer has an effect upon the experiment. As preposterous as it sounds, if a physicist is looking for *particles* of light, that is how light will present itself.

However, if the physicist is looking for *waves*, the light will take the form of waves. Thus there is no objective observer (at the subatomic level), since observations affect the result. It is as if the *intention* of the observer in a quantum experiment significantly, though mysteriously, affects the outcome.

For those who thought that the world was a rational and predictable place, these recent developments in physics (over the last seventy years or so) have been disturbing, to say the least. While the philosophical questions posed by quantum mechanics challenge the very bedrock of our cultural assumptions in the West, it may not be quantum physics alone that deals the death blow to our outmoded and, if I may say—*dangerous* ways of viewing things.

I have a very specific reason for inserting the word "dangerous" by the way. Recently the United Nations released a report on the environment saying that if the Earth were a human being, it would be in the critical care unit of a hospital. That is how dangerously out of balance our ecosystem has become. Our very existence is now threatened as a result of the technological advances we have created. We are polluting the Earth with such rapidity that many scientists are concerned that we may be on the brink of a biological disaster. This disaster is a direct result of the underlying philosophy in the West that basically views nature as something to be dominated and Earth's resources as something to be used by whoever gets to them first. Combine this domination philosophy with an ever-advancing technology, and we have a potent combination for catastrophe. Third-world countries, modeling themselves after the prosperous West, are decimating their natural resources in an attempt to "catch up." Unfortunately, many of these areas of the world hold the last remnants of the great rainforests, which are, along with the oceans, the greatest producers of oxygen. As these areas are deforested, we are losing hundreds if not thousands of species of plants and animals. Even more, we are also losing the biological generators of the air we breathe. Our cultural assumptions about our inherent right to dominate the environment have led us to the brink of disaster.

Something is going to have to wake us up collectively, something that cannot be questioned. And I believe that in the West, for better or worse, that something will probably come from the sciences.

I think that the cultural awareness of our situation and the need for immediate action may come from three distinct areas. The first of these is from the science of ecosystems, which is showing us how deeply connected is our own survival with the survival of other plant and animal species. We cannot indiscriminately decimate other species without damaging the biological fabric that sustains us.

The second area will come, I think, from quantum physics and its union with psychophysiology. Psychophysiology is a relatively new field that studies the interconnections between our mental experience and the neurological activity within our nervous systems. The union of these two sciences is beginning to reveal a world that actively interacts with our intentions. In other words, what you and I think and feel has an effect upon the world around us. We are not passive billiard balls *waiting to be struck* by reality; we are in some very real way *co-creating* reality from a myriad of possibilities through our thoughts and feelings. I think that within the next two decades, possibly less, there will be a growing cultural awareness that what we think and feel impacts both our individual and collective lives.

The third area of influence will, I believe, come from an area of science known as "subtle energy research." As more research scientists are exploring this fascinating domain, there are even professional organizations, such as ISSSEM (the International Society for the Study of Subtle Energies and Energy Medicine), dedicated to disseminating the latest breakthroughs. One of the central revelations of subtle energy research is that we are, from an energetic standpoint, like luminous eggs of light and energy. This description of "strands of light" and "energy vortices" within us is remarkably similar to some of the descriptions of our nature according to many indigenous shamanic traditions, traditions which span thousands of years and pre-date our scientific methodologies.

One of the breakthroughs in subtle energy research occurred in a laboratory at UCLA in Southern California. This landmark work was conducted by Dr. Valerie Hunt, a widely respected research physiologist and former professor at UCLA. Through her research (which is discussed in her excellent book, *Infinite Mind: The Science of Human Vibrations*), Dr. Hunt has scientifically measured and documented an energy field around the body. This field is highly sensitive and responds to stimuli even faster than the brain. What she calls the "field," the ancients called the aura. And through Dr. Hunt's work, this most ancient and modern of mysteries has entered the arena of scientific credibility since it can now be measured and quantified. Dr. Hunt has also documented energy centers within the body and recorded the sounds they emit. These major energy vortices within the body correspond to the chakras discovered by yogis thousands of years ago.

As other researchers join the quest to explore the body's subtle energies, a fascinating picture is emerging. Through breakthroughs in computer technology and imaging we are now gazing deeply into the inner world of our bodies—a world as wondrous as any galaxy.

Using these modern methods, researchers are beginning to map out some of the effects of emotions such as love and appreciation. It appears that whenever a human being experiences the emotion of unconditional love, a powerful intercellular resonance takes place that makes the DNA deep within the nucleus of cells more orderly. This is as potentially Earth-shaking to the purveyors of our current medical models as was Copernicus' view that the sun, rather than the Earth, was the center of the solar system. This revolutionary research will need to be duplicated by others before it becomes generally accepted, but the work holds great promise.

Another fascinating area of research in the effects of emotions on health and well-being is being conducted by the Heart Math Institute in California. The researchers at Heart Math have developed reliable protocols that can not only improve our psychoimmunological responses to stress, but also improve mental performance as well.

As a result of continual breakthroughs as significant as these in the field of subtle energy research, we are at the threshold of a major scientific revolution. If I may be so bold as to summarize some of the possible impacts of this emerging science, I would postulate three things. First, we are beings not only of flesh and blood, but also of energy and light. This energetic and luminous aspect to our natures obeys different laws than do our fleshly bodies, i.e., our bodies obey the laws of Newtonian physics—in other words, our everyday reality. Our energy and light bodies, however, are not bound by such laws, and are instead most accurately described by the laws of quantum physics. Secondly, as our culture comes to accept the notion of an energy and light component to our beings, I imagine that we will see a greater sensitivity to the effects of our actions, since to become aware of energy and light at a perceptual level automatically refines awareness. Thirdly, I imagine that we will see a great cultural increase in creativity such as we have not seen since the Renaissance. My reason for this optimisim is based on many years of observation, in which I have watched my clients and personal growth groups enter more creative ways of being and living after encountering their nature as energy and light.

If the three areas of science I mentioned earlier do actually come to fruition in the ways I imagine, our very ideas about reality and our human possibilities will be radically changed. It is an exciting time to be alive—if one can avoid dissipative stress. The theory of dissipative structures says that if you take a system—say a human being or a human society and subject it to stress, two things may happen. If the human or human society is strong enough, it will move up to a higher level of order as a result of the stress. If the system isn't strong enough, the stress will disintegrate the structure, resulting in physical or mental/emotional death.

In some ways, each of the major characters in our story is confronting his or her own dissipative stress. Each is finding an old world of set realities falling apart to reveal a world far more vast than they ever imagined. And in my opinion that is exactly what is happening to all of us. Whether we choose to be conscious of it or not is another issue.

The sciences are showing us a vastly paradoxical universe that is just as magical as it is logical. We may, as a culture, still insist upon holding on to our narrow mechanistic and materialistic view of things; after all, you may point out, it has served us for more than two thousand years.

But a new world is at hand, a world brimming with paradox and with possibilities beyond our imagining.

The characters you are about to meet are wrestling with this very new world. As I watched them come to life in the creation of this story, I came to love them. Something about them endeared them to me, and hopefully to you. The reason, I think, is simple. They are the stuff of which you and I are made.

As you enter this strange and mysterious fiction, know that the edges of reality and make-believe are fuzzy. I personally know people who have the odd abilities that the main characters possess. As a species, we are not at the apex of evolution as our schoolbooks would have us believe. Methinks we are just at the beginning.

Tom Kenyon
Orcas Island

CHAPTER ONE

His body had been floating for some time now, the only sound the faint murmur of air pumps feeding oxygen into the darkened tank.

Deprived of all sensory stimulation, Sheeb drifted in the pitch-black chamber, his mind quivering with the light of a thousand million hallucinations. At times he would rocket through the cosmos, at others he would tumble through some brilliant galaxy to find himself dissolving into an exploding nebula.

Hovering in interstellar space, Sheeb gazed at the remnants of the latest nebula only to be yanked out of his reverie by a neurological mutiny. The deepest and most ancient parts of his brain were not interested in his meanderings. They only wanted to know where in the hell his body was. As the cerebral cortex ejaculated yet another hallucination, the lower, more primitive structures of his brain were having a difficult time of it. One second Sheeb was standing on a cliff overlooking the ocean, the water whipped to a frenzy by mating sperm whales, the air heady with the scent of leviathans and salty spray. In the next moment, Sheeb was falling through the gaping mouth of a black hole.

Finally, the brain would realize that Sheeb wasn't standing on a cliff or falling through a black hole at all. He was inside an isolation tank in the bedroom of his penthouse apartment. His mind might have been off in the cosmos, but his body was safely floating like some preonate in its own watery womb, thirteen stories above the streets of Arlington.

At this rush of reality, Sheeb's lungs would fill with air and a sigh would pass through his lips. And then the hands would rise in the air, searching for the body in the pitch-black darkness of the chamber. The nerve endings in his fingers traced the familiar contours of his ribs and belly, finally resting where they were now, cradling his cock and testicles, floating like pale sea urchins in a dark and salty sea. Deep currents of pleasure reverberated through him.

"I'm safe; life is good." Sheeb smiled at the simplicity of neural logic as he let his hands drift back into the silky saltiness of the chamber.

Perhaps it was the random firing of a neuron, or an identification with the water in the tank, but suddenly Sheeb saw Susan staring back at him. His eyes popped open in surprise but the image remained unchanged. She was wearing a red beach towel, and her moist hair fell loosely about her shoulders. Sheeb felt her eyes steal into the deepest part of him, and he shuddered with pleasure-electricity as a cool breeze swept off the water across the boat. She motioned him to the back of the vessel, caressing him with her eyes. As Sheeb rounded the cabin, he noticed a blue blanket sprawled out on the floor. Ran stood shirtless... unzipping his pants, and smiling.

The hallucination changed. A large wave rocked the boat, and Susan fell over the railing into a churning sea. As in a nightmare in which everything moves in slow motion, Sheeb watched in horror, unable to move. He could not call out to her, as if his words might turn the tide in any way. Nor did she see the moving darkness as it came upon her.

She was looking up toward the light that filtered down from the surface as the hideous killer slammed into her. The water shook, and her body shuddered from the impact of its jaws. Fresh clouds of crimson blood swirled about her. Doubling over in agony, she caught a single glimpse of the monstrous shark circling her for the kill.

Her oxygen-starved lungs burned for air. There was the sudden taste of vomit at the back of her throat, and then—a chilled peacefulness possessed her as her lungs filled with water. Sheeb watched helplessly, unable to save her. Susan's world was ending. Time had stopped. Whole constellations of brain cells were dying in a carbon dioxide stupor.

Miraculously, the fear was gone. She looked with a kind of bemused detachment at her own blood as it pulsed from torn arteries draining the last of her life. Her eyes glazed over and her head tilted back. For a moment she floated eerily, like a torn marionette. Finally a single bubble of air rolled from her open mouth and rose silently to the surface. The last of her buoyancy now gone, Susan slowly drifted into the murky darkness below.

Sheeb trembled from the shock. The hallucination had cut too close to home. Why now? Why after ten years did the memory come back to haunt him?

As Sheeb contemplated the memory, music began to drift into the chamber. Schullerian's Requiem for Synthesizer and Vocastrati wafted from four speakers invisible in the darkness. His six hours were up.

Sheeb, mostly out of curiosity to see what it would do, had left the selection of the piece up to the house computer. Drawing from a collection of 6,000 digitized pieces, the computer had chosen, quite at random, the second movement of Schullerian's Requiem—the haunting Plutonian Explorer Dolorosa. Hailed by critics as one of the most significant accomplishments of the twenty-first century, Schullerian's work had found a large audience.

If popularity were a sign of anything, the Requiem had, indeed, developed into a major cultural obsession. But then, anything connected with the ill-fated expedition to Pluto was virtually guaranteed attention. It was as if the entire global society had become obsessed with what was, in truth, just another space accident. Something about the expedition to Pluto had gripped the imaginations of the world's inhabitants, seducing them into the dark and alluring planet of the underworld.

The Explorer had left for Pluto nine years ago, the four men and three women making their fateful voyage in cryonic suspension. While enroute to the strange planet at the edge of the solar system, the rocket motors misfired. The Explorer veered past its destination and hurled its crew, unconscious and asleep forever, into deepest dark space.

Schullerian, obviously moved by the event, had woven a lush and mesmerizing tapestry of sound and music. Only the Vocastrati could have captured the essence of this, his greatest vision. Developed only three years ago, the Vocastrati recorded the sounds of a human singer or chorus, routing them via microprocessors through the emotional center (known by neurologists as the limbic core) of the conductor's own brain. The conductor could then "attenuate," as it was called, the music to the vibrational patterns of his own feelings. The effect was startling, with entire audiences breaking down into sobs... as if on cue at the most moving passages.

The Requiem, now throbbing through Sheeb's own body, pulsed with such pathos that tears came to his eyes. He floated for awhile, listening to the charged emotions of the music, as a deep and insistent sadness began to stir within him. Another holomemory gripped his mind and body.

He was standing in the hallway at St. Jerome's orphanage. Spring had just come to Massachusetts, and sunlight was streaming in through the large glass windows. Sheeb stood there fascinated by the brilliant light and the sudden burst of warmth, but these were on the periphery for the small boy of four. He had just learned from Buck, one of the older boys, why he had been orphaned. Buck had snuck into the office and had read Sheeb's records. His mother was never coming back for him.

Buck Steele stood towering over Sheeb at the feet of the Blessed Virgin, paralyzing Sheeb with his rage. "Look, you little worm....the nuns think you're so wonderful..... bhlak!" Buck spit at the foot of the Virgin for emphasis. He must have caught the look of utter terror in Sheeb's eyes, for suddenly he seemed to calm down for no apparent reason. Buck ran an arm across his mouth where some spittle had clung to his trembling lip. Sheeb stood looking up into the large brown eyes of the older boy. Suddenly his body started shaking with a mind of its own. A tidal wave of despair filled him, and a strange sound, like a grief-stricken whimper, almost escaped from his gaping mouth. He swallowed the harsh feeling just in time. Two nuns had just stumbled in upon them.

Buck shot a final look of rage at Sheeb, who pretended not to notice as he greeted the sisters. He saw Buck slink away from the corner of his eye as he spoke to the nuns. Somehow he managed to talk, his voice sounding far away. It had been hard work to seal off such feelings—to feel unloved is a horrible thing. But he did it. And as he grew older there were moments when those deep feelings of loss would surface like a tired leviathan arching its back and diving again into the watery depths, but mercifully the moments would seldom last.

Sheeb returned from his holographic memories of St. Jerome's to the floating darkness of his isolation chamber. Schullerian's great Requiem was coming to an end, and Sheeb reached up through the darkness to find the door. As he pushed on the panel, a thin shaft of light sliced through the darkness around him. Throwing the door wide open, Sheeb rested his head on the ledge, luxuriating in the cool air that eddied in around his face and shoulders.

The stark nature of his holo-graphic memory fascinated him. Some memories were faint, like tracings in sand while others were intense and clear like the incident at St. Jerome's. How strange that the memory of child-hood angst would be so vivid after all these years. Was the pathos of the music responsible for such a response?

Taking a deep breath, Sheeb sighed and looked up at the ceiling. The Vocastrati had done a real number on him. Pulling himself out of the tank, he dripped saltwater onto the rug. He stepped into the shower and stood under the cold water until he felt himself coming back to his senses and the distressing memories fading.

Toweling himself off, Sheeb walked over to the computer display to see who had called him during his session in the tank. There were two messages. One was a computer call from Alfred Bach's office to confirm his briefing tomorrow morning, and to let him know that he would be meeting with Alfred Bach himself. The other was from Kathrina Jason on Christos.

Sheeb draped the towel over his shoulders as he reached for the phone. He had called Kathrina about a week ago when he saw that his work with Lowen was coming to an end, suggesting that they go off on a long weekend together. Kathrina accepted and suggested her place. Sheeb was ecstatic. Empaths like Kathrina had tremen-dous healing abilities that blossomed from a deeply intuitive and sexual nature.

Sex with an "ungifted one," a term used derogatorily by many Empaths to describe the average person, could never, and had never generated in Sheeb the bliss and ecstasy of riding the "Shakti current" that was generated from flows of sexual bliss created by internal energy circuits in the body. Empaths were adept at turning on these intoxicating pathways, and Kathrina was a true master of the art. Sheeb's body tingled at the prospect of spending time with her.

His fingers punched in the code to connect him with Christos, the small island where she lived. Sheeb looked out over the tree-dotted landscape of Arlington as invisible waves sought out a communications satellite in geosynchronous orbit. There was a faint glitch as the waves found the orbiting receiver/transmitter, and a slight bleep as the waves found Christos.

"Hello?"

"Kathrina?"

"Oh, Sheeb." Her voice sounded inviting. "You got my message."

"Yes, and I'd love to come down for a few days, if that's still on." Sheeb noticed that his voice sounded cooler and more detached than he felt.

"How soon can you make it?"

Sheeb could almost feel her in his arms once again. "I've got a debriefing with Alfred Bach tomorrow morning. I guess I could be down there sometime late afternoon. How does that sound?"

"Divine." Kathrina paused for a moment. "Oh, and Sheeb—"

"Yeah?"

"I've got a surprise for you."

7

"What is it?"

Kathrina laughed girlishly. "If I told you what it is, it wouldn't be a ..."

"Just one hint. Come on, Kat."

"Okay, just one. It knows you intimately well even though it has never met you."

"You can do better than that," he cajoled.

"Beggars can't be choosy."

Sheeb laughed. "See you tomorrow afternoon."

"Tomorrow afternoon."

There was a click, and the receiver went silent. Sheeb sat for some time, staring out the window. To let himself feel as deeply as he did for Kathrina was to open himself up to something he had closed off ten years before. "To cherish anything is to lose it." This maxim was always ringing in the back of Sheeb's head for in the smorgasbord of subatomic particles that Sheeb called his world, nothing lasted forever, not even the great spiraling galaxies, not the Schullerian Requiem, and certainly not love.

And yet Sheeb had to smile at himself as he leaned back onto the pillows, his hands tucked behind his head. His mind may have been confused and tentative about his feelings for Kathrina, but his body certainly wasn't. Somewhere deep within himself there was a force that continually drew him to her. That force, whatever it was, had been speaking to him; and although it spoke without words, although its grammar was made up of neurotransmitters and the flush of hormones, it spoke an ancient, eloquent, and most urgent language that every cell in Sheeb's body understood.

It was a messenger from the deep. And Sheeb had learned long ago to trust the great messengers that swam uncharted waters. But what he didn't realize, what he could never have realized lying on his bed in Arlington, was just how deep those waters really were, nor how deep he would soon have to swim. Had he known, he might never have left for Christos.

Sheeb's thoughts returned to the call from Bach's office. The Lowen case had been demanding, and tomorrow he would have to brief the enigmatic Bach himself. He had never seen the man, only heard of him. The arrangements for the project had been made through Bach's assistants. In fact, until today's phone message the briefing was to have been with Bach's staff only. Sheeb was never to have met the president of Biotechnologies. The world renowned financier lived in virtual isolation. Why then, did he want to see Sheeb?

Sheeb felt a disturbing uneasiness at the prospect, but couldn't quite figure out why. He tried to read, but the uneasiness persisted. Finally, after midnight, he laid his copy of "Spectroscopic Analysis of Mutating DNA" on the night stand, and turned off the light.

At 3:30 in the still darkness of early morning, he had a dream. He was stepping into an elevator that was to take him to Bach's top-floor office. The doors closed and the elevator rose at an alarming speed. At the 666th floor the doors opened, and Sheeb felt the air leave his lungs in a gasp of horror.

Ran was standing in front of him, naked and pressed against a huge black cube that hummed with a strange insect-like sound. His hands and feet had been bound and nailed to the front side of the cube as in crucifixion. Blood was dripping from his hands, streaming down his sides and across his belly. The small rivulets that swirled around his thighs had dripped down to his feet and formed a small puddle on the burgundy carpet. Sheeb stepped closer. Ran's eyes were fixed, as if in trance, gazing into some far and distant world. Sheeb looked down at the puddle forming from Ran's blood, and stepped back. Floating inside the vermilion sea, there were stars.

CHAPTER TWO

Kathrina stood on the balcony of her bedroom, pulling her rich auburn hair back from her eyes. Below her, the ocean caressed the nearby rocks with salty fingers. The setting sun, now a brilliant orange, poured light over a restless sea. The Precious Ones cavorted far below the cliffs, whistling to each other and inviting her to join them.

But for now her thoughts were far away from the dolphins and the dazzling water, jewel-like, before her. Kathrina pulled her arms about herself and caressed her shoulders. "What is it about him," she asked herself, "that haunts me so?" Her mind rolled over memories as the sea rolled beneath her—a whiff of pheromones remembered, the smell of Sheeb's hair seemingly carried on ocean breeze.

In her mind's eye, Sheeb stared back at her, a smile on his face. His lips called out to her, and she imagined his naked body pressed against hers. A pulse of pleasure turned into a deep yearning within her. Memories of the times they had been together floated past, and she sighed as a great wave of sadness slipped over her.

This time she knew that she might lose him. She had been hiding part of herself away, protecting him from its harshness, she told herself, but she could not do it any longer. The price of hiding was too high. It was better to live in loneliness, she reasoned, than to pretend some part of her did not exist.

Luna had made it all so very clear. On the beach under a starlit sky, Luna had spoken to her, her words borne to Kathrina on moonbeams. And in her unrelenting and strong love, the goddess had stripped away Kathrina's complacency, showing her who she was and what she must become.

Remembering that night, Kathrina pulled her hands to her heart. Tears of recognition came to her eyes. Already, awesome energies were pressing themselves into her life. Strange new powers of healing and seeing were opening to her. Nothing would ever be the same.

She could feel a new vibration pulsing around her, enveloping her in its mist. And whatever it was, it charged her with an energy that affected everything she touched. Remeira had broken down and wept in the garden when she first glimpsed Kathrina after the initiation. Walking down to the healing chamber that morning, Kathrina noticed that the precious ones had become unusually silent. Upon entering the water, the female dolphins encircled her as in an ancient ritual. Somehow they, too, had recognized the great change in her.

Shiva, one of the male dolphins, had brushed against her side despite warning cries from the females, and for three days he drifted listlessly in the water, refusing to eat. Occasionally he would whistle a low frequency that Kathrina had heard only once before, during the death throes of a porpoise several years before.

The female dolphins encircling Shiva would not allow Kathrina to enter the pool. Only Remeira was allowed to wade into the waters in vain attempts to force-feed their torpid male companion. During those three interminable days Kathrina could not sleep. Finally, on the third day, exhausted and feverish with fatigue, she fell into unconsciousness. At first it felt like falling into a bottomless abyss, but then she heard the sound of water, and then smelled the unmistakable scent of brine.

She had fallen into the sea and was swimming with Shiva through an unknown atoll. Around them the ruins of an ancient temple lay strewn across the sand. Light filtered down from above through the turquoise sea. Swimming through the ruins of this other world, Kathrina had the feeling she had been here before. Her limbs tingled from an unseen energy. Gliding through a coral-encrusted archway, Kathrina noticed strange ovoids made of pink marble, shaped like large eggs. Strangely, she seemed to grow stronger in their presence. The water seemed thicker, like amniotic fluid, and Kathrina had the distinct impression she was swimming through a gigantic womb. Looking over at the dolphin she noticed that he was in trouble, his strength quickly ebbing away. Death was near. The sudden realization stunned her. Shiva could not follow her. To do so would destroy him. A different kind of power was required here, in the temple of feminine mysteries.

She must guide him back to the opening through which he had followed her in. Swimming over to her friend she stroked his head and gently turned him around, guiding him out from the ruined temple. As they passed through the archway that they had first entered, Shiva suddenly regained his strength. Kicking himself through the water with his flukes, he disappeared into the light that poured down into the water from above. Kathrina turned to the archway and passed once again into the ancient temple—alone.

That was the last thing she remembered. Hours later Remeira was knocking at her door with news. Shiva had recovered. The gift, or curse, from Luna (the perception depending on Kathrina's mood) had been to reveal the mysterious temple in Kathrina's dreamtime. Now a powerful magnet, it continued to call her. And the deeper

Kathrina penetrated the temple within her mind, the more the strange powers of the place poured over into her outer world.

Her telepathic and healing abilities were escalating. Luna's gift was pressing her to the edges of her known world. How much awareness and how much power could she contain? And how would those she loved survive her metamorphosis? One of her closest dolphins had nearly died from it. And what would happen to her as she continued to surrender to the strange new powers? There was no way to know; there was nothing to do but continue.

Her thoughts turned back to Sheeb. How would he react to Luna? Would he stay or would he leave when he glimpsed this other side of her? This much she was sure of—she could no longer conceal the vastness she was becoming. To do so was now impossible.

If Sheeb stayed, a part of him would have to die. And if he could not find the strength to die to what he thought he was, then he would leave her—must leave her to save himself.

CHAPTER THREE

$\int$heeb stepped into the egg-shaped vehicle and took his seat by one of the windows. Other passengers claimed their spaces as the electromagnetic motors of the transport began to murmur their low-frequency dialogue to the central computer. A panel light at the front flashed: Fasten Safety Belts. The automatic doors pulled closed, nestling themselves into the sides of the aluminum steel mother.

The brakes released with a slight rocking motion and the transport surrendered to the magnetic pulse that would hurl it into the distance. Sheeb felt his body pushed back into the upholstered chair as the transport rocketed through the plastishield tube. The world became a blur. Sky, earth, and steel of buildings flashed by in a vortex of light. A long streak of green told Sheeb that he had just entered Park East on the border of Maryland. The panel at the front of the speeding egg noted arrival time in 3 minutes 15 seconds.

Sheeb glanced over at a mother with her two sons. The four-year-old was holding a model of the Plutonian Explorer, turning it in his hands as he flew through his imaginary world of galactic space. His mother was gazing out the window as her youngest son, a few months old, suckled at her breast. The four-year-old looked up at his younger brother and at the unattended breast hidden beneath his mother's sweater. His free hand soared up through space and lightly touched the nipple that nudged at the world through the soft garment. His mother's hand slapped his thigh.

"Stop that! I've told you a hundred times, I don't like it when you do that."

The boy's hand returned to his lap and the idle spacecraft. For an instant he looked back at his little brother with an unbearable and unfathomable rage. He turned and caught Sheeb's eyes, and sensing something mysteriously wrong, he returned his attention to the model spacecraft and zoomed off into outer space, far from this world, searching for the glimmer of new and distant galaxies.

The rushing sound of the tube turned into a low alternating hum as the pulse brakes labored to slow the transport for docking. Seconds later the electromagnetic motors nudged the vessel onto the loading platform. The side doors slid out from their nesting places and a computerized voice spoke to the departing passengers.

"Thank you for riding InterCity Transport. Have a good day."

The passengers poured out from the egglike vehicle like so many strands of DNA disseminating themselves, their passions, and their dreams into the human sea of Bethesda. Sheeb hailed a street shuttle, and ten minutes later he was riding the elevator to Alfred Bach's office, which covered the entire top floor of BioTechnologies. After Sheeb passed through two security checks, he was shown into Bach's personal museum, which served as headquarters for one of the most powerful financiers on the planet.

Sheeb was told to wait in Bach's massive office. The head of BioTech would be with him shortly. As he ambled across the deep pile burgundy carpet, Sheeb's eyes came to rest on one antique and then another. A half-million years of human and pre-human history were enshrined within these walls, each object lovingly displayed on its own pedestal. Here was a porcelain from fifth-century Manchuria, and there the fossil remains of a woman with child from the mid-Neolithic era. The skies of Spain exploded into a cobalt fire as Sheeb looked at a painting by El Greco. Nearby the cold weightiness of stone had been transformed by Rodin into the vaulting passions of two lovers' embrace.

The objects and priceless works of art had been arranged so that they formed a corridor through the burgundy sea of Bach's office, so that anyone entering to see him had to walk the long pathway lined with the relics of past centuries. Finally the long corridor ended and Sheeb stood facing a large mahogany desk inlaid with platinum, an exquisite piece which he recognized immediately. The massive desk was completely barren except for a folder. Sheeb turned his head so that he could see the title page. It was the report he had sent in on Lowen.

"Psychoneurological Evaluation of Abram Lowen, Ph.D., for BioTechnologies, Inc. Attn.: Alfred Bach." Sheeb noticed that someone had stamped TOP SECRET: CODE 1 in the bottom right-hand corner. That could mean only one thing, Sheeb thought, as he walked to one of the oversized windows that looked out over Bethesda: a Computer-Assisted Mind Scan. Lowen had been one of their top scientists before his abduction. Whoever had taken Lowen hostage had gained access to crucial information, information that BioTechnologies had intended to use to create new products. And new products meant money for its stockholders.

Such information in the wrong hands would enable another company to compete with BioTechnologies on its own exclusive turf as the world's foremost genetic recombinant engineering firm. It was only natural that BioTech would want to know just how much Sheeb had been able to learn about Lowen's project. Sheeb smiled at the thought of the burning question in the minds of his inquisitors. Just how much does he know?

The answer almost made Sheeb laugh out loud. He knew everything. Every thought, every feeling that Abram Lowen had ever experienced had been laid open before Sheeb's sensitive eyes as he "tracked" Abram's mind in the terrible aftermath of the Deep Mind Probe.

Whoever kidnapped Abram had gotten what they were after. The DMP uncovered virtually every secret project Abram was engaged in. Such information could be sold for millions of dollars to the right bidder, and there were probably a dozen or more major corporations eager to pay almost anything for a chance to compete with the Giant BIOT.

What outraged Sheeb was not the questionable morality of stealing information. After all, most conglomerates were in the business of stealing everything they could. What bothered him was the way in which the information had been retrieved. The Deep Mind Probes were only used by those who lacked the ability and the finesse to "track" their subjects, and often resulted in irreparable damage.

And even when there was no damage to the neural pathways, as in Lowen's case, there was a horrible aftermath of amnesia and dissociation. When Sheeb met him, Lowen did not know his own name. He did not remember his wife and two kids. In fact, his last memory was spending the afternoon in Yankee Stadium with his father at the age of nine.

During the first few weeks of work, Sheeb noticed that Lowen would often dissociate from his body. One afternoon during a session, Lowen was explaining, in heated excitement, how certain enzymes remove the outer walls of cellular tissue. In the middle of the conversation, Lowen asked Sheeb in a hushed whisper how he could possibly know such information. Lowen listened attentively as Sheeb outlined to him the facts of Lowen's background—graduate of Columbia...Mensa... Nobel Laureate...BioTechnologies.

Lowen was completely unaware that his own hands were unbuttoning his shirt. By the time Sheeb had ended, Lowen was nearly naked. When Sheeb pointed out to him that he had taken his clothes off, Lowen broke down and wept. It was this kind of neurological nightmare that the Deep Mind Probes left in their wake. And it was for this reason that Sheeb would never forgive the Mind Thieves.

The flip side of that, of course, was that the existence of the Mind Thieves made it possible for Sheeb to demand the exorbitant fees he charged for his services. After all, a rehabilitated top research scientist is a precious commodity to an employer.

Shaken from his reverie, Sheeb turned to see Alfred Bach emerging from behind a Persian screen. As he crossed over to Sheeb, Bach pointed to his desk.

"Excellent report, young man... very thorough. I like that." Bach's handshake was firm. Though Bach was reputed to be 135 years old, Sheeb guessed him to be in his late 50s.

"Geriatrics."

"Beg your pardon?"

Bach laughed. It was an inviting laugh, but it left no doubt about who was in charge. "I thought you were trying to guess my age."

"Well, I suppose I was. You know there's a rumor that you're 135."

The air in the room seemed suspended by a slender smile that etched itself across Bach's face. "It's not a rumor." Bach motioned Sheeb to a chair in front of the desk and seated himself behind the massive work of art.

"I have access to the best geriatrics in the world today."

"Is that why you bought BIOT?" Sheeb asked.

Bach nodded.

Motioning to the desk, Sheeb said, "It's not every day that you see an Amoretzi in someone's office."

Bach grinned. "It's not every day that you meet someone who knows an Amoretzi when he sees one, either. I take it you like his work?"

"He's a genius."

Bach leaned forward. "I agree with you, as to your question about BIOT... I bought out the company when it was just an infant, three PhDs in a basement laboratory working on the recombinant engineering of DNA." Bach raised his right hand to his chin and looked Sheeb straight in the eye. "And do you know what our first product was?"

Sheeb shook his head.

"Biodegradable drain cleaner." Bach chuckled. "From drainpipes across the planet to this!" Bach spread his arms as if to encompass the entire office. "When I purchased BioTechnologies the idea of extending life span was just beginning to be taken seriously. I knew in my gut that it was possible, but there was no systematic exploration of the discipline. I diversified BIOT into several different areas, each one creating salable products that made us a multibillion dollar company. And part of every dollar, I funneled into research. We fathomed the unfathomable sea of human genetics, tagging every bit and piece of the great DNA helix."

Bach looked heavenward as he spoke, his body wrapped in an emotional fervor, like an evangelist swaying to an unseen heavenly choir. "There were long periods of desperation, such as I could never describe...months of research ending at a doorway that wouldn't open. But finally,"

Bach's hands shook as he rolled them into fists, "even nature had to yield her secrets."

There was a fire in Bach's eyes as he spoke, as if some galactic inferno within were giving birth to a new sun. As Bach continued talking, Sheeb dropped into alpha state, the energy surges in his brain suddenly coming into a slow, rhythmic pulsation. Sheeb turned his attention to Bach and dropped into sync with Bach's nervous system. Slipping into sync was like diving into the summer swimming pools of Sheeb's youth, the cool water sliding around him, a deep calmness beneath the surface overtaking him as his legs kicked him deeper into the watery depths.

Floating in the misty calm of alpha, Sheeb scanned the energies coming from Bach's presence. It was like tracking a supernova. He had never experienced so much intensity coming from one man. It was as if Bach were an ancient star exploding into the eternal darkness of space. Some inner fire was driving the man, driving him to something Sheeb couldn't quite uncover without going deeper. And yet with all that intensity there was the faintest hint of sadness coming from the heart of that exploding sun. It then came to Sheeb. Here on the top floor of BIOT, one of the most powerful men on the planet lived surrounded by a half-million years of relics, so much human history stretched out before him like some vast sea. It was as if each object in that room held the silenced voices, the vaulting passions, and the lost dreams of all humanity that had walked before him.

"Do not go gentle into that good night." A shred of poetry written by a 20th Century Welsh poet shimmered from Bach's brain into Sheeb's captivated mind. Bach's accomplishments challenged the gods, and yet atop his modern Olympus he was alone with no one to share his deepest passions and haunting fears.

Sheeb now understood why the financier had taken time to talk with him before the actual interrogation. Like some lonely quasar in the eternal night, Bach was sending signals. "Am I alone? Do you understand my loneliness?"

Sheeb's intoxication with his sudden realization was interrupted by the intercom on Bach's desk. A hidden panel slid from the right side of the desk, revealing a highly sophisticated command center.

"The technician you sent for has arrived, sir."

"Good, send him in."

Moments later the door at the end of Bach's office slid open and a nondescript man entered the room carrying an attaché case. As the man approached Bach's desk, Sheeb saw that the case was, in fact, a portable microprocessing unit, the type used for a Computer-Assisted-Mind Scan (CAMS). Sheeb was fascinated by the man walking toward him through the corridor of relics, through a half-million years of human history. Walking past the exquisite objects that flanked him, past the exploding skies of El Greco, even past the mummified boy from Pompeii, the man didn't so much as turn his head.

As the man stepped up to the desk, Bach waived him to a table at the side of the room. The man nodded and proceeded over to the interrogation area to set up his equipment, which took less than five minutes to prepare. Sheeb sat at the small table while Bach lowered himself into a nearby couch. The technician's skilled hands attached electrodes to Sheeb's forehead. Sheeb sensed something he didn't like about the man, and dropped into sync with his interrogator as the technician adjusted some dials on the instrument.

The technician was mildly paranoid. He had not been Bach's first choice for this assignment. A lot of his energy was being consumed by trying to do everything right. It was easy, therefore, to slip past the normal censors into the deeper strata of his consciousness. A cool, vacuous blast struck Sheeb as he entered the man's deeper self. The man was almost entirely mental. Barely conscious of his body, he lived in a world where everything was thought out and carefully calculated.

But what struck Sheeb most was that the man was devoid of feeling. It was as if he had become an automaton, a mere extension of his own microprocessor. To live without passion is to live the life of a subhuman. Sheeb had been running into more of these types lately, and it bothered him.

"Are you ready yet?" Bach asked. There was an edge to his voice. The technician answered looking down at the floor. "Yes, sir."

"Good, let's get on with it." Bach raised his arm and reached over to a small set of buttons on the table next to him. For a moment his hand wavered in the air, and Sheeb noticed the barely noticeable palsy in his hands. Someone else might not have seen it. Bach's fingers found the panel and he spoke into a hidden intercom. "Send them in."

The door at the other end of the office slid open and a man and a woman stepped onto the burgundy carpet. Their white robes sweeping the floor gave the illusion that they were floating, not walking, toward Sheeb. Enthralled, Sheeb watched their every movement as they approached him. They were obviously Empaths, with the purple sash around their necks indicating that they were Scanners as well.

Interesting, he had known employers to use either CAMS or Scanners, but he had never seen both used at the same time. Both were equally capable of detecting if he was withholding pertinent information. Why, then, would Bach employ three people for the same task?

As the two Empaths drew closer, the technician bristled with barely concealed contempt for the two intuitives. The woman and young man upon arriving at the interrogation area nodded to Bach and looked past the technician to Sheeb, a movement of the eyes that was slight, yet all encompassing.

Looking into the woman's eyes, Sheeb had the strange sensation that he was gazing into infinity itself. The woman registered no emotion—neither cold nor warmth, neither acceptance nor hate. She had already dropped into trance and was moving into the Empathic Void. Her sensuous lips and deep auburn hair reminded him of Kathrina. For a moment he could smell the salt spray of Christos.

As the two figures hovered nearby, Sheeb took a closer look at the young man. Obviously Eurasian, had it not been for the slight almond shape to the eyes, he could have passed as a Roman god come to life in the hands of a Michelangelo. As Sheeb looked into the piercing green eyes, he found himself slipping into sync despite himself. The Empathic Void was like a magnet that pulled everything into itself, and the skill of a Scanner was to weave the void so that there was no escape.

Bach motioned the two to take their places slightly behind and to either side of Sheeb's chair. It was a sudden feeling, like a breeze through an open window. The Scanners were slipping their energy fields around his brain. The slightest movement in the waters of his mind would attract attention, and every thought in his mind would be caught like a fish strangled in their nets, now cast into the neural pathways of his brain.

The woman raised her hand.
"We are ready."

As he fine-tuned the CAMS, it was obvious the technician resented the presence of the Scanners.

The spontaneity and sexual powers of the Empaths made him uneasy. Despite his distaste for the technician, Sheeb found himself feeling sorry for the man.

The technician's voice sounded mechanical and far away. "Ready, Mr. Bach."

Bach ripped into the dossier, questioning Sheeb on every aspect of the seventy-two-page document. After two and a half hours he was satisfied. Dismissing the technician and the Empaths, he motioned Sheeb to stay put. As the Empaths left the room, Sheeb followed them with his gaze. The haunting face of the young man turned and for a moment looked back at Sheeb. A chill ran up Sheeb's spine as the Empath suddenly disappeared, leaving Ran in his place. For an instant, his old friend stared back at him. The vision dissolved as quickly as it had appeared, and the young man with almond eyes turned to leave, the door closing behind him.

The voice was casual. "Could I interest you in a glass of wine?" Bach spoke from behind a bar in the corner of the room. From the way he was cast in shadow, Bach seemed to embody both Dionysus and Hades, raised from the dead, inviting Sheeb into the dark and forbidding underworld.

CHAPTER FOUR

Sheeb took the glass of Lafite Rothschild from Bach's outstretched hand. The financier's palsy was becoming more obvious. Following Bach to the couch, Sheeb compared the dark color of his wine to the lush richness of the burgundy carpet beneath his feet. Bach lowered himself into the couch, suddenly seeming older.

Sheeb sat across from him in an overstuffed chair, and posed the question that had been bugging him since his encounter with the Empaths and the Mind Probe. "Can I ask you something?"

"Certainly," Bach leaned back against the plush fabric of the sofa.

"Why did you use both the Empaths and a Computer-Assisted Mind Probe? Either one is effective by itself."

Bach smiled, "Artistic persuasion and a philosophical query."

"How so?" Sheeb asked, genuinely intrigued.

"I developed the habit of getting more than one opinion on important issues when I was in my early twenties. I have found that experts rarely agree, and by having more than one view of a situation, I am better able to make an intelligent decision. The other reason is that I am fascinated by the juxtaposition of technology and human perception. The fact that both the technician for the Mind Probe and the Empaths agreed that you were not withholding information was a comforting agreement between two very diverse ways of working. And I suppose the final reason was to amuse me. If you noticed, the Empaths had an instinctual loathing for the technician. He, in turn, resented the presence of the Empaths. I found the tension between the three to be amusing and an odd kind of aesthetic, like the stilted roles of the Japanese Kabuki Theater. The situation would not allow for them to express their dislike of each other openly, so instead, their mutual distaste revealed itself in the how they moved and looked at each other, as well as the timbre of their voices and their choice of words."

"How do you see their discomfort as theatrics?" Sheeb asked.

"Oh no, Mr. Sheeb," Bach waved his wine glass through the air. "Not theatrics, style."

"Style?" Sheeb repeated incredulously.

"Yes, style." Bach nodded.

"How so?"

"I admit that style is often viewed as a merely surface phenomena, like what is trendy and vogue. But true style is an expression of the individual, and when true style is present, it reveals the inner emotional timbre of its creator through the most minute of gestures. For instance," Bach leaned slightly forward, "did you notice how the Empaths pretended to not be ruffled at the technician's presence?"

Sheeb nodded and smiled.

"They are, by the way, two of the most highly skilled Scanners I have ever worked with. But, like most Empaths, they have learned to conceal their real feelings in social situations. As a result, they were attempting to hide their tension by pretending to be cool and detached. But the gesture of their eyes was too perfect to be genuine. They were definitely acting. They could not, in their station, say anything so they kept their genuine feelings concealed, but the style of their movements betrayed their contempt. I found their artistic manner at hiding the truth to be admirable, and I found their pretense to be amusing.

"Extraordinary," Sheeb took a sip of his wine and sighed.

"So now my turn." Bach reached into his jacket, "How did you... ah... develop your fascinating abilities?" It was an act that any magician would have coveted. The hand slipped a small capsule from Bach's vest pocket to his tongue within a heartbeat. Most people would not have noticed it. Sheeb could hardly believe it had happened. As Bach sat there inquiringly, the shaking hands steadied. Moments before, small waves had crested across the surface of his wine. The tiny sea was now still, and Bach looked at Sheeb intently, waiting for his answer.

"Well, Mr. Bach, I..."

"Call me Alfred. After all, we share a common love—Amoretzi." Bach raised his glass in the air.

"As I was saying, Alfred, it's a long story."

"I've got all the time in the world." Bach sipped from the fluted glass.

"I'm afraid I don't. There's a hydrojet waiting for me at Port."

Bach sighed, and looked into his glass as if he were searching for something beneath the surface of his wine. "Well, I can understand schedules. Still....a few minutes would be nice, that is, if you don't mind."

"I would be honored, Alfred."

"Why would you say that?" Bach seemed mildly irritated.

The great quasar within the man was sending signals again. And like an interstellar satellite, Sheeb decided to leave the small, familiar orbit of Alfred Bach, the employer, entering instead the unknown space of the fellow human sitting across from him in the darkening light. The hydrojet could wait for a bit.

"When I walked into this room," Sheeb sipped from the ruby sea imprisoned within glass, "I didn't believe what I saw."

"Yes, go on." Bach's deep brown eyes burrowed into Sheeb.

"Alfred..." Sheeb took a deep breath and continued. "When I saw this room, I hadn't met you yet, but I already admired you. I knew..." Sheeb took another sip from his glass, "that here was a man who understood the poignant significance of history. Not only that, but here was a man with an obvious depth to his nature, and who displayed it with style.

Bach smiled, took a deep breath and sighed. "It's not every day that I run into someone who understands the concept of historical significance. Nor do I find many who appreciate my... as you say it... style. I've always thought that if you can't do it with flair, why do it at all? Bach stared at his wine for some moments, and then looked up at Sheeb. As for my depth, I don't like to waste my time in the shallows. How about you?"

"What do you mean? Sheeb asked.

"Do you prefer the depth or the shallows?"

Sheeb looked at Bach quizzically.

Bach leaned back in his couch and stared at the large window to his left. "The question isn't fair without context, so let me be a little more precise." Bach turned and looked directly at Sheeb. "I have another job for you, and it has more depth and historical significance than you could ever imagine."

"When would it start?"

"Immediately."

"I'm afraid not." Sheeb swirled the wine in his glass. "I'm leaving for Christos this evening, for a long, long over-due vacation."

"A moment ago, you said something quite interesting... you said that history was poignant. I couldn't agree with you more. That's why I think you'll change your mind when you hear what the assignment is. It is, after all, filled with both pathos and history...our..." Bach paused momentarily to be more dramatic, "...future history, that is." Bach looked down to the carpet in silence.

"OK, Alfred. I don't guarantee anything, but go ahead." Sheeb leaned back in his chair, cradling the glass of wine in both hands.

"All right, I'll make it short." Bach leaned forward and precariously perched his wine glass on the edge of the couch, a mocking challenge to the force of gravity. "We recently acquired a new consortium out of Germany. The company is called Hellenstat and is primarily a manufacturer of microprocessors. Their research team has developed an organic matrix micro-processor. It has tremendous potential, due to its minute size."

Sheeb sniffed at the fermented aroma in his glass, and for a moment his mind wandered to images of grapes hanging on their vines, plump and waiting to be plucked. "It sounds pretty lucrative. What's the problem?"

"If that's all there was to Hellenstat there wouldn't be any problem, but it's not. For some reason not clear to me, management decided, a few years ago, to underwrite a special research project. The stockholders didn't even know about it."

"What was it?"

"It's called the MWM Project, or Mind War Machine."

Sheeb set his glass down on the table next to him. "What exactly does this Mind War Machine do?"

"It interfaces with the psychic abilities of its operator to create a distortion in the time-space continuum. It can then transfer an object or group of objects into a totally different dimension."

"Objects... you mean things like war satellites?" Sheeb asked.

"Yes, and the first preliminary test of the device has been successful. They managed to 'translate,' as they call it, a small cube of carbonite."

"Jeez..." Sheeb raised a hand to his mouth. "Where does it go.... when they translate it, I mean?"

"They don't know."

Sheeb grunted and looked out the window, following a rain cloud as it drifted by in the invisible air currents. "Alfred... which do you think is larger.... the universe or human stupidity?"

Bach chuckled. "Both are infinite, Sheeb."

Sheeb turned his eyes from the rain cloud to the man sitting in front of him. "But I don't see what this has to do with me. I'm not a detective."

Bach stood up and walked over to one of the windows, his back turned to Sheeb. As he stood silhouetted against the backdrop of darkening clouds that had moved in over Bethesda, his voice turned somber. "After the successful test of the MWM the head of the research team became very depressed. He is reportedly catatonic. He won't talk or eat."

"How about the others on the team. Why not ask them how it works?"

"No one knows how it works. They were purposefully kept in the dark."

Sheeb reached for the last swallow in his glass. "So you want me to go out there, wherever there is..."

"California," Bach offered.

"You want me to go to California and work with this guy to find out how the MWM works and return that information to you, right?"

"Correct."

"I'm sorry, Alfred. I wish I could help you out, but that Lowen case took a lot out of me, and I promised myself a vacation. Why don't you try one of the other deprogrammers?"

"None of them are as good as you and you know it."

"I appreciate the compliment, but you're still going to have to get someone else."

"Oh... I almost forgot to mention one more important piece...the pathos I alluded to earlier."

Sheeb didn't like the tone in Bach's voice. Bach was still facing the window to the darkening sky. "I believe you know the chief researcher, the one who's gone catatonic..." Bach turned and faced Sheeb, his eyes cutting into him like a laser. "His name is Randal Farr. I believe you know him as Ran."

Something lurched in Sheeb's throat, and he thought that he was going to get sick. "Did you say Ran Farr?"

"Yes," Bach replied nonchalantly, "I believe you went to school with him at Stanford." Bach turned back to the window to watch a fork of lightning blaze across the horizon. "Weren't you two roommates?"

"Yes." Sheeb raised his hands to his mouth, a gesture meant to still the anguished cry from deep within. His body seemed heavier, as if gravity were dragging him down through the chair and into itself. He could still hear Bach's voice, but it sounded far away.

"Of course, you don't have any further obligations to me or the company." Bach walked back to the couch and sat down across from Sheeb. "But I thought you might want to help your friend."

Sheeb sighed and looked down at the floor. "I haven't seen or heard from Ran in ten years. I didn't even know if he was alive."

"What happened?" Bach asked, a sudden tenderness to his voice.

"I don't know that I want to talk about it."

The holomemories were painful enough, but to see Ran again.... Sheeb couldn't imagine. After the accident and Ran's disappearance, he dreamed about him for nearly two years. The dreams were always the same. They always occurred in strange places, and Ran would always ask the same question: 'Why?' But the dreams had mercifully stopped a long time ago, and had been replaced by a kind of numb emptiness. Could he, would he bear the pain of seeing Ran again?

"As you wish, but I need your decision."

"I need some time, Alfred."

"We haven't got much. I can only give you 24 hours."

"OK, I'll call you from Christos."

Bach walked over to his desk and tapped a button. A hidden computer console slid out from the side of the Amoretzi, and Bach asked for Sheeb's portable phone number. Having entered the number into the computer, Bach turned to face Sheeb.

"There's something else I should tell you," he said.

"Yes?"

"The carbonite cube must be retrieved before we can close down the project."

"Why?" Sheeb asked.

"It concerns dimensional physics, and I don't pretend to understand this kind of thing. However, according to our top people, 'translating' the cube could have a negative impact on the flow of time and history in this dimension. It has to do with chaos theory, since the smallest movement of energy can eventually create massive changes—especially when moving from one dimension to another."

"Yes," Sheeb said excitedly, "like the idea about the butterfly beating its wings in the Amazon, how it alters the air pressure immediately around its body which could, under the right circumstances, create a thunderstorm thousands of miles away."

"Exactly," Bach added.

"So, Alfred, under what circumstances will the cube alter time and history?"

Bach shook his head. "We don't know, which is why it must be retrieved. We can't take chances."

The room suddenly blazed with a flash of lightning, and a moment later, the low rumble of thunder shook the air, indicating that the storm was overhead. Bach stepped toward the balcony. "Do you mind if we step outside? I like thunderstorms."

"Why not?" Sheeb stood up and followed him onto the suspended terrace. Outside the skies had turned black, the wind whipped to a fury as lightning flashed all around them. The horizon had turned blood-red, a mixture of light from the setting sun and the frenzied lightning.

Bach leaned against the concrete railing, looking like an ancient gargoyle peering up into the heavens. Stretching his arms across the still-darkening sky, Bach pointed to the lightning that was slicing the heavens.

"Look at that power, Sheeb!" he said excitedly. The palsy had started to return to his hands again. Deftly slipping another capsule under his tongue, the old man steadied himself against the railing as he waited for the medication to take effect.

As Bach stood silhouetted against the darkening sky, Sheeb dropped into sync and tracked the man into the pulsation of neurotransmitters coursing throughout his brain. Within that vast sea of neural pathways, an electrical storm swirled from the deep motor areas of the brain, spiraling on itself like an intercellular hurricane. Shreds of neurotransmitters with important information from the muscles of Bach's body floated helplessly in the froth and foam of the storm. Nerve endings within the brain waited for impulses from the hands that would never arrive. And in the neurological turbulence, the tsunami of Bach's anger added to the fury of the storm.

Finally the medication pulsed through the great arterial spring, and the hurricane within his brain was silenced into a whimper. Neurotransmitters lost in the turbulence now found their way to waiting synapses spreading like fingers in the biochemical sea.

Sheeb slipped out of alpha back into his usual sense of himself and observed Bach looking out across the turbulent sky, his hands still once again. But Sheeb knew this to be only temporary. Within weeks Bach would be dead.

Alfred looked over to Sheeb, his eyes moist with emotion. Sheeb leaned against the railing and looked back at the financier.

"You were right, Alfred. We don't have much time, do we?"

"You were tracking me just then, weren't you?"

Sheeb nodded.

Bach grinned, obviously pleased with himself. "I knew it... I could feel it."

Sheeb turned to see him better. "Alfred, why put so much energy into this Mind War Project when the end is so near?"

Bach laughed, his dark eyes suddenly turning cold. "First of all, my friend, the end is not as near as you think. I've beaten the thief you call death before, and I will outsmart him again. Right now every researcher in BioTechnologies is working on a cure for this, this..." Bach's hands moved through the cool air like a falcon searching for prey, "this condition."

Sheeb stepped back a bit. "I'm sorry, Alfred. I didn't mean to upset you. It's just that if it were me..."

"You'd what?" There was challenge in Bach's voice.

"If it were me, I'd want to spend time with myself and with friends."

Bach looked Sheeb straight in the eye. "I don't have many friends, Sheeb. People bore me. Their stupidity and petty concerns have long since lost their ability to amuse me. And their tragedy," Bach shrugged, "the tragedy of being human, of which I am one, is that we are born into this universe only to be taken away from it. Our bodies are made of dust from stars long ago lost. And out of this dust we live our lives." Bach raised his hands to his face. "With these eyes, Sheeb, I see the world... I can love what I see or I can hate what I see, but I can see! I have tasted the sweetness of Equa fruit, which in my mind, Sheeb, in my mind reminds me of the musky moistness of my lover Heleina. It seems like only days ago, but it's been over a century since I last saw her. I tasted her, Sheeb... I heard her voice... made love with her and felt myself deep within her... so deep within her I thought that I would surely die. But it wasn't I who was to die... it was her. A minuscule defect in her DNA killed her."

Bach leaned against the railing. "The irony is that today we could easily correct such a problem, but a hundred years ago we had no idea what to do. And another irony is that I can still hear her; I still see her. But she is not here anymore. She is here!" Bach held his head as if holding a reliquary. "She lives only in the electrical patterns of my holodreams, my memories, and when this star body dies, the entire world dies, and so does my Heleina, at least for me."

Bach turned and faced the wind, his eyes afire with an inner brilliance. "Whatever birthed me into this world will have to fight to take it away." Bach raised his arm and pointed to the sky now heavy with rain cloud. "Out there, beyond those clouds, stars are being born. And all those stars must someday die. Their great burning hearts hurl photons and fire into the night. And for all their magnificence, they will all be methodically extinguished, their light never to be seen again." Bach leaned his head back, and looking upward took a deep breath. "And I know the star killer, Sheeb. I feel it in my own body. It pulls at my chromosomes. It would, if it could, scatter me like so much dust across the face of this planet." Bach's fist struck the railing. "I will not give in to entropy, Sheeb, I will fight the star killer. I won't give in to the hell hole of gravity. I won't lie down and surrender to that thief of death."

Bach paused and stared at the street far below. "I'm sorry. I didn't mean to bore you with my impassioned speech."

"I wasn't bored, Alfred."

Bach looked over at Sheeb, his eyes searching.

"In fact," Sheeb said, "I'd like to propose a toast to your next hundred years!"

A slight smile of amusement slid across Bach's face. "There is a bottle of champagne in the wine cooler next to the bar, glasses are underneath. Bach turned and faced the raging sky.

As Sheeb poured the bubbling wine into the two glasses, he was aware of an emotion surfacing through the waters of his consciousness. It moved like a warm breeze from his heart and up into his throat. Placing the glasses on the marble bar, Sheeb glanced out at the man standing on the terrace, braced like Captain Ahab searching the ever-darkening sky. The great quasar within Bach had called out and touched the heart of Sheeb.

CHAPTER FIVE

The eerie green light from the terminal flooded across Alex Vollen's desk and onto the floor where he was doing push-ups. Accelerating his pace, Vollen lowered his body to the floor, his taut belly brushing the fur rug. Even through the bearskin, he could feel the cold draft from under the floorboards.

The terminal flashed a communiqué, grabbing Vollen's attention.

SHEEB TO ACCEPT CONTRACT. BE PREPARED TO ENACT HELLENSTAT PROTOCOL. FUGUE ONE OUT.

Vollen grunted, raised himself from the floor and walked to the luminous screen. Punching in the letters with one hand, he rubbed the hard muscles of his chest with the other. "Acknowledged. Runner out."

Vollen pulled a dossier from the middle drawer of his desk and continued on into the next room. Laying the folder on a wooden table, Vollen sauntered over to the stove and poured himself a cup of coffee.

Catching a glimpse of himself in one of the frosted windows, Vollen resembled a Norse god come back again to life. Short-cropped blond hair fell just above his ears in small curls. Aquamarine eyes returned his stare, and as he gazed at his own reflection he felt a familiar sense of pleasure.

Lowering the coffee to the table, he turned his attention to the dossier. Who was this guy named Sheeb that Fugue had become so obsessed with? The top-secret papers had been delivered by special courier only days before.

Vollen took another sip of his coffee and sat down at the table. Pulling the dossier from its folder, he spread the papers out and looked at Sheeb's photograph. He sensed something odd, something in the eyes…not the color of the eyes, no, nor was it the shape of the sockets. It was something deep within the pupils. It was something he had never seen before, something he did not understand, the mystery of which intrigued him.

Laying Sheeb's picture back on the table, Vollen picked up his cup of coffee and stared out the window at the brilliant moon now flooding the valley. A slice of the mercurial light cut across Sheeb's picture and Vollen fingered it, amused at the thought of time unfolding before him, carrying him inexorably closer and closer to this man named Sheeb. He had no way of knowing what Fugue wanted of him, no way of knowing what he would, in the end, have to do with or to Sheeb. And the unknowingness of this aroused him.

Walking over to a window, Vollen looked out through the frosted glass to a star posted in the frigid night. The lone cry of a wolf echoed through the valley. Vollen's breath stopped, his ears listening intently through the silent air. Off in the distance, but not very far, the cries of a pack answered the loner. Vollen's blood rushed to his head. Barely able to contain his excitement, he pulled off his jeans and sat on the floor.

He barely felt the cold of the Bavarian night radiating up through the wooden floor and into his buttocks. Already the bellows of his lungs were doing tumo, the inner fire. Practiced by Tibetan hermits high in the Himalayas for thousands of years, tumo allowed adepts to live at high altitudes in a land dominated by snow and ice. Vollen had learned the secret practice from an exiled lama in Nepal while on a trek years earlier. With deep breaths, Vollen fired the furnace of his gut as he meditated on an inner sound, a secret mantra given him by the Buddhist hermit, and soon, very soon, his body was impervious to the cold.

Stepping outside, and closing the door behind him, Vollen stared up at the dark sky and the moon. Transfixed by her luminous glow, the Nordic god of his body seemed raised from its silent winter grave, steam pouring from his nostrils like a beast set free from dark stillness.

Vollen reached down and rubbed snow over his naked body, his laughter echoing through the trees. The cold could not touch him. The wolf pack had heard him, and called their lupine cries into the night. Hearing their voices, his heart was suddenly pierced by an unbearable ecstasy. As he bolted into the trees, the moon washed over him, its silver white light dancing and sparkling off the virgin snow.

The moon followed him, or so it seemed, into the forest, where Vollen could sense the wolves resting. Over a frozen stream, through a narrow tunnel, Vollen could feel them closer. He could almost taste them.

Over there, in one of the clear- ings, a small pack of wolves was rolling in the snow, three females and a male. The male seemed young, probably just whelped last spring.

Crouching behind one of the smaller boulders, Vollen could smell musk, the pheromones from their thick winter fur drifting on crisp, cold air.

As the wolves rolled over each other and nipped the air, Vollen felt overcome with a yearning to join them, a deep calling in his blood pulling him to crawl out into the clearing on all fours, urging him to join the pack. Only a shred of sanity in his mind prevented him from acting on his impulses.

Vollen breathed deeply into a sudden sadness. He had always felt it, for as long as he could remember—the never-belonging. Even among men he was alone.

Startled by a sudden noise, Vollen turned to see an avalanche of snow falling from the branches of a nearby tree. The wolves bolted up on all fours, teeth bared, eyes searching the air. The young male stared back wildly. He had seen him.

Vollen felt his blood dropping into his stomach. Growling, the male slowly and cautiously padded his way over to the naked figure crouched in frozen snow. The rest of the pack followed closely behind, snarling, white-hot breath pouring from their nostrils.

As they approached, Vollen felt a deep calmness coming over him, a quickening in his loins he had never felt before, a sharpening of the senses. Dropping down onto all fours, he slowly crawled toward the approaching animals.

The male stood still, looking at Vollen intently, his teeth bared in the mercurial light of moon-beam. Stepping past the motionless male, one of the larger females inched forward. Not more than two feet away, Vollen's steamy breath mixed with the wolf's own panting. The jowls that had been pulled back to bare her sharp white teeth now dropped forward. Sniffing him, she drew slightly closer.

Rolling onto his back, Vollen exposed his belly in the universal sign of submission. Upon him now, she sniffed the naked flesh of his stomach and chest.

Her pack, puzzled, kept their distance, still not clear about what they should do.

The young male sided up beside the female and began to sniff Vollen for himself. As he sniffed down toward his belly, Vollen reached up and gently stroked the head of the female who was now at his face. She backed off slightly with a simple look of curiosity.

Vollen could feel the warm air from the male's muzzle against his skin, as it followed his smooth belly down to his sex. The male suddenly backed off and growled at Vollen, his teeth bared ominously. Vollen instinctively pulled his hands up over his stomach. His mind raced. For a moment he could almost feel the wolf lunging for his belly, pulling his steaming guts out over the virgin snow.

There was a growling up near his head, and suddenly it was over before he knew what had happened. The female leapt into the air in front of the male, knocking him to the ground. Enraged, he attacked the female, but she was larger, and in her cunning she stayed just outside his reach. Frustrated, the young male ran to the edge of the clearing and, raising one of his hind legs, pissed on a tree. Turning, he leapt into the undergrowth, the rest of the pack following.

The she-wolf stared at Vollen for a moment before leaving to catch up with the pack. For a moment, as he returned her gaze, it seemed to Vollen as if time had stopped, the earth, around them, standing silent and still.

For only a second he closed his eyes, but when he opened them again, she was gone. Pulling himself to his feet, Vollen trekked back through the snow to his cabin. The heat from the tumo was beginning to wear off, and Vollen could feel the frigid air against his skin.

CHAPTER SIX

Off in the distance Sheeb could see the curtain of rain behind him. Bethesda and the eastern United States lay somewhere beyond that gray veil, but out here the sea reflected the late afternoon sun like millions of diamonds thrown across the surface of the water.

He had rented a Mercury Class One hydrojet, rejecting the agent's offer of a Class Two at half price. Only the silver rocket was equal to his sense of adventure. The autopilot adjusted the speed and altitude of the craft with exquisite precision, the waves rolling beneath him long and sluggish. The Mercury rocketed three meters above the surface, its short stubby wings pulling lift from invisible air currents.

At present speed, Christos lay about an hour away. Sheeb flipped a switch on the luminescent panel in front of him, stealing control of the vessel from autopilot.

"All right, Merc, let's see if you can do everything they say you can." He shoved the attenuator forward, and the hydrojet's nose dove straight for the water below, like a heron dropping for prey. Water exploded over the front ports and over the slick back of the plummeting craft. The brilliant light of late afternoon turned blue-green as it slid beneath the surface into the deep waters of the Caribbean.

The ocean floor lay far beneath him, a murky, ever-darkening blue. Pulling the attenuators to the right, Sheeb arched the Mercury onto her side and slipped through the water like a giant manta ray, the only sound the throb of thrustpulsers.

Off in the distance Sheeb could see the swift climb of the ocean floor that led to canyons of extinct volcanoes. A flash of light spread across his peripheral view. A school of dolphins was following him, their white backs reflecting light that filtered down from the surface above. Sheeb let them swim past him a bit.

Pulling back again on the attenuator, he nosed the craft up towards the surface, the thrustpulsers catapulting the hydrojet upward into the air like a breaching whale. Sheeb leveled her off at thirty meters. Below him the school of dolphins shot through the water, breaking the surface, the air around them filled with smoky plume.

"So far, so good. Now let's see..." Sheeb reached over to the luminescent panel once again, and flipped on the plosion jets. The words were hardly out of his mouth when he was knocked back into his seat by the force of acceleration. The rear plosion jets screamed as they rocketed the Mercury through the air like a missile, forcing the air from Sheeb's lungs. Instinctively, Sheeb pulled back on the attenuator and the craft slowed down and dropped low into the water. Christos now lay ten minutes away.

Sheeb flipped on the autopilot and walked to the rear of the compartment. From the sudden acceleration, the plastishield had come loose. Sheeb stepped up to the large sphere and inspected the bindings that held it in place. One of the buckles had snapped open. Pulling it tight, Sheeb checked the others.

The plastishield was a rescue sphere fully equipped to handle the immense pressures of the ocean floor. A giant transparent bubble, it could hold two fully grown adults, either floating them to the surface when set free from the hydrojet or lowering them into the depths, if so desired. Haunted by an odd feeling he couldn't name, Sheeb lashed the large womb-like vessel in place.

The hydrojet suddenly slowed down as a warning flashed from the autopilot. Sheeb rushed forward to the command station. Christos lay off in the distance shrouded in mist. The autopilot, programmed never to operate the vessel at high speeds near land, had slowed the Mercury to a slow crawl. Sheeb slipped into his seat, and took control of the craft once again. Arching the Mercury onto her side, he guided the hydrojet to the far side of the mysterious island where Kathrina's villa nestled itself by the sea.

As he drew closer, Sheeb could see the crystal spire of the healing chamber nestled in the fronds of palm trees. Slowing the craft down as he approached the docks, Sheeb flipped another switch and the Mercury skimmed the surface, as Sheeb cut the engines. The hydrojet coasted up to the side of the docking area, and Sheeb jumped onto the dock.

That was strange. On the other side of the platform an alpha shuttle sat floating in the water, its metal skin reflecting the orange and reds of the setting sun. As Sheeb tied the hydrojet to the platform, he noticed Remeira walking up the path toward him. Her dark eyes sparkled in the reddish light, her black hair falling about her shoulders. She smiled as she neared the platform.

Born to a Jamaican sorceress, Remeira had spent the last three years with Kathrina, learning the skills of Empath and healer. Something had changed since he had seen her last. He could see it as she drew closer. It was in her eyes. An inner spring had been tapped. The young woman had an air of serene assurance about her, as if a great river that had been dammed within her being was now sure of its journey.

Remeira stepped up to Sheeb and put her arms around him, pulling him close to her. She held him for a moment and then pulled back, her hands still about his waist. "Sheeb!" Her eyes glistened with feeling. "So good of you to come, we have missed you. I'll show you where you are staying the night." Remeira took his hand.

"Where's Kathrina?" Sheeb asked.

"With a client. He came in unexpectedly. He's on contract." Remeira glanced at the ground. "She had to see him."

"How long?" Sheeb asked, unexpectedly peeved.

"I don't know for sure." Remeira eyed him as she talked. "You look tired. Why don't we go to the healing chamber?" Sheeb nodded. The debriefing with Bach and the news about Ran had been pulling at him. Floating in the chamber would be wonderfully relaxing.

Walking through the palm trees, Sheeb watched the last rays of sunlight reflecting off the crystal spire of the chamber. A crescent moon hung in the lapis sky as clouds reflecting the dying light of day drifted off near the horizon. Remeira opened the door to the round building, letting Sheeb inside. Closing the door behind them, she motioned him to the center of the pool as she walked over to a panel of switches by the far wall. There was a low hum coming from above. Sheeb looked up to see a large crystal descending from the ceiling as violet blue light filled the chamber from recessed lights. Soft music drifted through the air.

Slipping out of his clothes, Sheeb entered the pool of warm water, fragrant with the sweet smell of the sea. The pool was constantly circulated with water from the ocean. A large channel gave access to the holding tanks where Kathrina's "Precious Ones" swam, fed, and communed with their human caretakers. Free to go wherever they wished, most of the dolphins chose to stay, if not permanently, at least for long stretches of time. Sheeb smiled as he remembered Adrian, the playful year-old who had befriended him on his last visit.

As he leaned back into the flotation supports, he asked Remeira where Adrian was.

"Gone." Remeira disrobed and entered the pool, wading toward him. "He left shortly after you returned to the United States." Placing one hand over his heart, Remeira held her other hand above his head. "Breathe," she said.

Sheeb took in deep breaths and let them glide out of him, the music and water carrying him ever deeper into trance. He could feel Remeira weaving the energies of his body as he luxuriated in the warm breezes she moved in and through him. Like magnets, her hands swept above his body, their growing intensity reaching deep into his tissues, pulsing life-giving essence into every cell.

Remeira stood for some time, weaving energy into Sheeb's body until, drawn by the energy of his pleasure, two of the Precious Ones entered the chamber. They swam around Remeira and Sheeb in wide, slow circles, occasionally brushing up against Remeira's thigh or Sheeb's back, and filling the air with their cracks and whistles.

"We'd better leave," Remeira whispered into Sheeb's ear. "Our friends are getting aroused."

It was true. The underbellies of the dolphins had turned bright pink, and they had become more insistent in their movements as they brushed up against their human playmates. Slipping out of the floating supports, Sheeb slid into the water. For fun he dove to the bottom of the pool like a dolphin, watching a ballet of air bubbles from his lungs rising up through the watery space.

The two dolphins circled Sheeb, their bellies bright with oxygen-filled blood. Shakti slid to the bottom of the pool and between Sheeb's naked thighs. There was a sudden rush of pressure as her tail whipped the water into a frenzy, shoving Sheeb towards Shiva.

Sheeb pushed himself toward the surface, the muscles in his thighs kicking through the blue-green water. He broke through the surface and pulled in a sweet, cool breath of air, the hemoglobin in his blood turning suddenly brilliant red. Cells anxious for the life-giving gas now breathed easy.

Sheeb turned to Remeira. "If I didn't know any better, I'd say those dolphins are after me."

"What makes you think they're not?" Remeira's eyes looked deep into him.

"It's just that I..." Sheeb coughed up some mucus at the back of his throat. "I know they're not *after me*, after me. I mean, I know I'm safe. It's just that I had this odd feeling down there."

"Yes?" Remeira arched her eyebrows.

"It felt like... Well, it felt like they wanted me sexually."

"As I said," Remeira tilted her head slightly to one side, "what makes you think they're not after you?"

"Come on Remeira, I can't imagine doing it with a dolphin!"

Remeira seemed suddenly aloof. "I thought you understood energy, Sheeb, since you presumably work with it in your job, but I can see I was mistaken. The Precious Ones are attracted to your energy. It excites them." Remeira pulled herself out of the pool, and reached for a towel. "I've got to go now. I assume you know where the guest cottage is."

"Yes, I remember."

"Good. That's where you'll be staying tonight. If you want to stay in the pool longer, make sure you're out within an hour. I have to do an energy clearing before Kathrina works with her client tonight." Remeira turned and walked toward her clothes, dressing in silence and leaving without a word.

Shiva and Shakti peered at Sheeb from across the pool, their bulbous heads sticking out of the water. Shakti whistled into the air, drawing Sheeb's attention. He looked to her side of the pool and caught one of her blue-green eyes. It seemed to Sheeb that she looked at him questioningly, but what was the question?

The music that Remeira had turned on suddenly shifted into a deep, haunting passage: Schullerian's Requiem. A chill ran through Sheeb's body. Shakti clicked and dove beneath the surface of the pool and slid over to Sheeb. The hairs on his legs stood on end as Shakti brushed up against his thighs. Instinctively, his hands reached down and stroked the dolphin's side. Turning over in the water, Shakti bared her bright belly. For a moment Sheeb hesitated, his conscious mind uncomfortable with his feelings and with what he thought was happening. But there was something deeper within Sheeb calling him, and in that moment it seemed as if the calling were coming from within his own body.

Small galaxies of human DNA spiraling about themselves were reaching out to their galactic brothers in the bodies of the dolphins now swimming around him.

In that moment of non-thinking, the great calling was urging him to swim deep into those waters from which the dolphins spoke to him, waters that mystified and terrified some part of him. But now the calling was greater than the fear.

Sheeb dropped into sync and slid beneath the water, his feet kicking him to the other side of the pool where Shiva and Shakti floated together. Sheeb brushed the underbellies of both dolphins and shot toward the surface, doing a flip as best he could. Instantly the two dolphins were swimming beside him, and Sheeb felt his body enfolded between the bioforce of the two animals.

His body tingled, and as he tracked the minds of the dolphins, he felt as if he were falling through a vast canyon of purest white light. Shakti nudged his chest with her bottled nose, and a shiver shot through his heart. For a moment he was no longer in the pool. He and the two dolphins catapulted through space, a canopy of stars all around them, and beneath them the Earth floated like a bubble in the interstellar sea.

The two dolphins arched onto their sides, swimming through starlight. Sheeb floated between them. Off in the distance, Sirius waited. Sheeb knew, without knowing how he knew, that this was their home. He could feel their excitement at his having recognized this most unexpected truth about them. Then, without warning, they turned a flip and the three of them were swimming down toward the turquoise oceans of missa gaia, Earth herself. As they drew closer, Sheeb felt something unfolding within his heart, for suddenly he could sense the life force pulsing from the great planet...pulsing from every bit of life...pulsing from the smallest protozoan to the mammoth sperm whales now feeding in the frigid waters of the Arctic...pulsing from the rain forests of Madagascar to field mice in Iowa...and with every heartbeat Sheeb could feel in himself the same power that drove the whales to summer feeding grounds, and sprouted seeds into redwoods.

The great gift of life seemed more precious than Sheeb had ever imagined. And the joy of it consumed him. Shiva and Shakti dove into the waters beneath them, and Sheeb opened his eyes to find himself back in the healing chamber. Tears fell from his eyes as he looked at the two Precious Ones across from him in the pool. The air tasted sweet, every sensation a feast, every thought a miracle.

The door to the healing chamber opened and Remeira stepped inside. Sheeb had forgotten the time.

As Remeira turned to face the pool, her expression changed. For a moment she seemed to swoon. Her eyes glistened with feeling, and a slight smile slid across her lips. "I apologize, Sheeb. I underestimated you. Please forgive me."

"What's to forgive?" Sheeb shrugged and both dolphins whistled. Pulling himself out of the water, Sheeb walked over to Remeira, water dripping from his naked body. Looking into each other's eyes, they both smiled.

CHAPTER SEVEN

The guest cottage sat at the edge of the compound. From Sheeb's window he could hear the sound of waves sliding up onto the small sandy beach. Outside, stars unfurled themselves across a cobalt sky, the great canopy of lights slowly winding its way to the far horizon. By morning Orion would be gone.

Unpacking his things, Sheeb walked over to the low-slung dresser against the bedroom wall. Setting his shirts into the open drawer, his eyes caught a flash of cerulean blue in one of the collars. He fingered the fabric, feeling the weft and weave, a softness to the touch, and a glimmer of blue to the eyes. It reminded him of Shiva and Shakti, that haunting blue of their eyes.

His mind raced back to the healing chamber and the journey he seemed to have taken. Sheeb knew the effects of deep trance, had witnessed himself flung off to far places before. That was, of course, the only possible explanation for what had happened with the dolphins. Perhaps it was the energy field they had surrounded him with, perhaps it had simply been those eyes, but whatever it was, he had been thrown into a kind of trance, and all the visions of the planet and all those feelings had just been the result of a deep hypnosis. There could be no other explanation, he told himself. And yet something remained to haunt him; something had reached deep inside of him and try as best he could, he couldn't shake it off. It clung to him, reminding him of something he couldn't quite remember.

Finally unpacked, Sheeb walked over to the library and flipped through the stack of holodiscs lined up beside the holocube. Grabbing a presentation of Genetic Star, Sheeb slipped the small disc from its holder into the translator. The three-foot cube of ebony carbonite hummed as lasers cut ribbons of color through the cubic space of the viewing area. Hidden within the three-foot-high stand, a series of lasers pulled signals from the translator, recreating the images and sounds of the original performance. The presentation had become notorious for its use of live human eggs and sperm.

Outraged by this act, the Catholicas, an extremist offshoot of the Church of Rome, had condemned the performance and its creators. One thing continually frustrated the Catholicas however, and that was the immediate popularity of virtually anything they condemned. Thus the performance of Genetic Star had minted millions of dollars for the six physicists who had created the group.

The ebony cube hummed as hidden lasers created a large spiral, the huge helix of DNA seeming to wind its way upward into infinity. The sound tidal-waved itself through the room, as subwoofers pulsed low frequencies into Sheeb's body. It felt to him as if every cell vibrated to the music now surrounding him. Routed through six vocastraties, the music from Genetic Star had been attenuated by the feelings of all its creators, en masse. It struck Sheeb like an angelic choir, its ever-ascending voice trumpeting praise for the Great Helix from which all living things come.

Superimposed on the ever-spiraling helix, three male performers walked into the viewing area as if suspended in mid-air, their white robes gently swaying. Cradling their gold and platinum chalices, the three men carried the reliquaries to a marble table, like priests from some distant time. Setting the chalices down in front of three electromagnetically sensitive microphones, the mysterious figures lowered the long-necked stands into the mouths of the receptacles. Suddenly the great roar of swimming sperm filled the space of the symphonic choir, their frantic sound reminding Sheeb of rocket motors.

Stepping up to the table, three women, also wearing white robes, placed chalices of their own next to the men's goblets. As they lowered their own long-necked microphones into the chalices, the cascading choir was now filled with the sound of three human eggs. Like an enormous heart the eggs pulsed their low frequencies into the growing choir, each pulsation of the eggs exquisitely recreated by the subwoofers. As each cell in Sheeb's body tingled to the frequencies that filled the room, he had a vague remembering. In his mind, Sheeb floated in the great intrauterine sea of his mother. Rubbing his shoulders, Sheeb stared into the moving holograms.

Lifting their chalices into the air, the three men gazed into the eyes of their priestesses. The rim of the chalices touched as the frantic sperm were slid into the waiting goblets, the three eggs pulsing the air for their genetic messengers. The images of the men and women faded as if turning into ghosts, their ephemeral bodies disrobing each other. Stroking and kissing each other, the women reached down and caressed the men's organs, which were uncoiling like snakes into the air.

Giant images of the three eggs floated into view, the three living planets gently swaying before the Great Helix as thousands of flagellating hedonists swam across the holosea toward the spheres. The eggs opened themselves to three of the Olympian swimmers, and quickly closed the doors to their inner sanctums.

As the sound of electronic trumpets and kettle drums filled the air, the exhausted sperm inside the eggs unfurled themselves like dandelions caught in the wind. The frantic pace of mitosis had begun. Outside the walls of the three pulsing eggs, a flotilla of unused sperm float-ed, dying in a sea of hololight.

There was a knock at the door. Flipping off the holodisc, Sheeb walked across the room and opened the door into the night. The soft light of stars, sent to earth a million years in the past, flooded the doorstep. Sheeb flipped on the light. It was Kathrina.

Reaching out for his hand, she stepped into the room. "Sheeb." Her voice sounded warm and soft. He pulled her close, her luscious breasts pressing against his hard chest. He drank in the odor of her hair. Running his fingers to the nape of her neck, he gazed into her eyes, the turquoise blue of them enfolding him.

Looking into her that way, Sheeb sensed something different in her. In fact he had noticed it as she stood on the doorstep drenched in starlight, something both unspoken and powerful.

"You've changed," Sheeb said.

"So have you." Kathrina gently stroked his temples, noticing the few gray hairs since last they met. Everything is always changing, Kathrina noted to herself. She walked into the middle of the room. "Remeira tells me you had an experience with the dolphins." She turned and faced Sheeb, her rich auburn hair falling loosely over her shoulders.

"Yes, I guess you could call it that. I prefer to call it hypnosis."

"Hypnosis!" The tone in her voice gently mocked him, though her eyes still seemed soft. She continued, "What makes you so sure that it wasn't real?"

"We've had these discussions before, Kat. The whole thing is just a function of brain physiology, nothing more."

"Sheeb, I have no issue with brain physiology, but I don't think things begin or end there. Whatever the truth of your experience with the Precious Ones, if it touched your heart, isn't that all that matters?"

"But it wasn't real. There is no way to objectively verify the experience, Kat."

Cocking her head back, Kathrina struck Sheeb like a great lioness preparing to jump her prey. "Who are you to know what is real or not real? I find it fascinating that you can work in the field that you do, and still insist upon your narrow perspective. How can you be so sure of your position? You know that our physical senses detect less than one percent of the known electromagnetic spectrum. Sheeb, that's like wearing a pair of blinders and insisting that you see the entire picture. Your intellectual objectivity is an illusion, an absolute illusion." She turned and faced him squarely. "And so is your materialism."

"I live by logic, Kat." Sheeb shifted his weight to his right foot and took a deep breath. "Without it, I would feel lost in this weird world. And although my experience with the dolphins was extraordinary, I put it all under the heading of mental experience—nothing more, nothing less. And finally, even though our mental experiences can sometimes be beyond words to express, I believe that they have less to do with reality than we would hope, and more to do with our unconscious desires and agendas."

"The Precious Ones showed you something immensely important, Sheeb, and whether you believe it or not is immaterial. They were calling you, my love. They were calling you to a new world, one vastly different than the one you live in day-to-day. Remeira was right. You saw it, and more importantly, you felt it. And no matter what logical bullshit you try to run it through, it has touched you." A single tear fell from her left eye as she gazed intently into the eyes of her lover. Her voice lowered to a whisper. "You can never go back...no matter what you do."

She threw her head back and looked up at the ceiling. A smile slid across her face and she laughed. Then Kathrina looked into his eyes, her words warm and inviting. "Oh, Sheeb, you can never go back."

CHAPTER EIGHT

It felt like someone had set off a small depth charge inside of him. Feeling the waves of emotion rippling through his chest, Sheeb recognized the truth of Kathrina's words. Although his mind raced to deny what she had said, in his heart he knew she was right.

For the longest time it seemed that he just stood there looking at her. Although his eyes told him the world was still the same as it was before, he had the distinct sensation that the furniture in the room had suddenly begun to float in the air, as if gravity had just given way to some greater power. Sheeb felt his throat swallowing saliva. His eyes focused on Kathrina's neck, and suddenly he wanted to kiss her, to ravish her, to swallow her. In his mind he could taste her. He felt blood beginning to pulse into his sex with each beating of his heart.

Kathrina looked into his eyes and smiled. "I brought you a present."

"You're the only present I want."

"Later." Kathrina smiled. "I won't be through with my client until around dawn. I'll come for you then,"

"You promise?"

"Promise." Her voice sounded lush, like the palm trees outside.

"So what's the present?" Sheeb asked.

Kathrina closed her eyes.

Dropping into sync, Sheeb followed her. She was calling something, but what? The image of a black Labrador floated through his mind. It was running on the beach. Sheeb could hear the roar of the surf. The animal rounded a large boulder, and Sheeb could see that he was nearing the guest cottage, perhaps twenty yards away. "He's almost here," Kathrina whispered.

Moments later the dog was at the open cottage door. He paused, looking into the room, his tongue barely protruding through his teeth. Kathrina motioned him in. "It's okay, Centauri, come on in."

The dog padded into the room and looked up at Sheeb. Cocking his head to one side, he barked softly over and over, his tail wagging the air. Walking over to Sheeb, the animal looked up at him with deep brown eyes. Looking down at the animal Sheeb felt something moving inside of him. He could still see Centauri looking up at him, but there was also a second image in his mind. He was looking up at himself through the eyes of the dog.

"Oh my god!" The words broke through Sheeb's lips. "He's a Valkovian Labrador."

"Yes." Kathrina said with pride.

"But Kat, they cost a quarter of a million dollars, assuming you could even find one."

"Actually, the current going price is three hundred thousand, but...Centauri was a present from a grateful client."

"My god, what did you do for him?" Sheeb asked.

"I helped save his daughter's life," Kathrina explained. "She had advanced leukemia. The medical doctors had given up on her."

"And you healed her?" Sheeb asked, kneeling down to feel the Valkovian's thick, rich fur.

"She healed herself. I just helped her see that she could do it."

Sheeb's finger's caressed the dog's ears as he looked up at Kathrina. "Kat, I don't know what to say. I... I've always had this fantasy that one day I'd own a Valkovian, but how did you know?"

"I know a lot more about you than you realize." Her words were as soft as the sea breeze that had just come in through the open window. Centauri sniffed the air and then licked Sheeb's face.

It was a warm feeling in the middle of his chest. There on the floor with Centauri, Sheeb felt like he had turned four years old. His mind shifted back to a holomemory. He had just asked his mother for a dog. She hit him, saying that she had enough to deal with without getting an animal. It was a few weeks later that he was taken to the orphanage. He would never see his mother again, nor would he ever have a dog. Sheeb felt a lump in his throat as he looked into the dog's eyes.

Kathrina walked over and gently touched Sheeb's shoulder, "I've got to go now, but I'll be back."

Sheeb looked up into Kathrina's moist turquoise eyes. A serene smile had etched itself across her lips, and in her face, Sheeb could see her deep love for him.

In that moment, standing in the doorway, bathed in the light of stars, Kathrina seemed to be the most beautiful woman in the universe.

CHAPTER NINE

Closing the door behind her, Kathrina left Sheeb alone with Centauri. The dog nuzzled up closer and stared into his eyes. The specially cloned Valkovian Labradors were world-famous, highly telepathic and predisposed to form deep bonds with their masters. During the cloning process each animal was imprinted with the sights, sounds, and odors of its potential master or mistress, thus explaining Centauri's deep emotions upon meeting Sheeb for the first time. He looked to be almost a year old; Kathrina had obviously been planning to give Sheeb her surprise for some time.

Centauri sat perfectly still, and Sheeb had the uncomfortable sensation that the dog was sizing him up. He had also never experienced so much unconditional love from an animal before. The Valkovians were famous for their empathic abilities in addition to their enhanced telepathic powers. It felt odd to be just sitting there while the dog's deep brown eyes burrowed into him.

Sheeb raised himself from the floor and walked toward the door. "How about a walk?" Centauri pricked up his ears, sat up and barked.

Sheeb opened the door, and Centauri followed him out into the night. The moon was just rising above the horizon. Stars blanketed themselves above, and the faint white glow of their burning surrounded Sheeb and Centauri in ethereal light.

Sheeb breathed in deeply, the salty smell of sea breeze in the air. Centauri ambled along just ahead of him. Deciding to play with the animal, Sheeb dropped into sync. Centauri turned around and looked into his eyes. It was an odd feeling, the shifting within himself. Suddenly he was seeing himself through Centauri's eyes. The cottage sat behind him, off in the distance.

Picking up a stick, Sheeb threw it into the air. "Fetch!" Centauri bolted off into the darkness, barking excitedly. Standing there, Sheeb had two distinct sensations—aware of watching Centauri as he chased the stick, and chasing after the stick himself. Through Centauri's senses, the earth seemed richer than Sheeb had remembered it. A symphony of sounds, smells, and feelings flooded into Sheeb's mind as he tracked the dog into the night.

The breeze filled his nostrils with the faintest hint of hybrid orchids as Centauri padded his way over to the sandy beach. The stick was falling now, dropping from its arc that had cut the sky. Sheeb sensed Centauri's muscles contract as the dog leapt into the air and caught the stick in his mouth. Standing there, Sheeb clearly felt the sensation of holding something between his teeth. The impression was so strong, he reached up to see if anything was there. There was nothing.

Centauri rounded a boulder and for a moment was out of Sheeb's sight. It was a strange sensation, not being able to see the animal, while images and sensations still floated in. Sheeb walked toward the boulder to check out whether the images he was seeing were correct or not.

Suddenly he felt himself peeing in his pants.

"Shit!" Sheeb reached down to his crotch but it was dry. Rounding the boulder, he saw Centauri pissing on a large rock. Sheeb leaned back and laughed.

Watching Centauri with his hind leg raised in the air, Sheeb suddenly remembered Ran, a holomemory firing through his mind. They were both drunk. Dawn was a few hours away as they staggered through the streets of Berkeley. At each fire hydrant, Ran pulled down his pants and tried to piss on it, wobbling back and forth, howling into the air like some berserk coyote.

Suddenly Sheeb felt intensely alone. His best friend had disappeared years ago, and he had tried his damnedest not to feel the hurt. But the truth was Sheeb desperately missed him, and now standing alone with Centauri, he felt small and insignificant. The sea breeze that moments earlier had felt refreshingly cool now felt cold and uninviting. Sheeb rubbed his shoulders and turned to walk back toward the cottage.

Centauri followed, every now and then brushing up against his master's legs as if trying to comfort him. As they walked back, Sheeb looked up into the vastness of the night sky. The words surprised him, as if they had come from someplace far away. "Oh, Ran... we're all just specks of stardust." Images of nebulae and dying quasars floated through Sheeb's mind. Sighing, he stepped up to the door and opened it, his body heavy with sadness. The relentless force of gravity, always present, seemed suddenly stronger.

Letting Centauri in behind him, Sheeb closed the door and walked into his bedroom. Stripping off his clothes, he glanced at the digital on the night stand: 2 a.m. He was under the covers before he realized that Centauri had curled up beside him in the bed. Surrendering to fatigue, Sheeb stroked his dog and drifted off to sleep.

Drifting downward into deeper levels of consciousness, Sheeb watched as clouds, pink and orange, floated through his mind's eye. The occipital area of his brain was shifting from the waking state of beta into the relaxed and floating feeling of low alpha. Drifting even deeper, Sheeb slipped into Dreamtime. His inner world opened before him, where images mimic the outer world but possess a strange and awesome power.

Off in the distance, on the sandy beach where he and Centauri had played, Ran stood naked, looking up into the starry night. Rubbing his thighs and belly, Ran looked at Sheeb and laughed. "Stardust, isn't it wonderful?"

Sheeb felt himself suddenly catapulted into deep space, light exploding all around him. He could no longer see Ran. All that remained was his laughter. And finally, quickly fading, even that was gone. Everything had disappeared and Sheeb floated, it seemed forever, in the still dark void of deep delta.

Outside, the stars made their long pilgrimage to the far horizon. The moon fell behind the sea, its silver rays shimmering from the back of a dolphin giving birth to her son, gently nudging him up to the surface to breathe. Within the healing chamber, Shiva and Shakti swam in long, slow circles, sensing the new addition to the web of dolphin life.

From deep within the void of sleep two images floated into Sheeb's mind. He followed them upward to the surface of what seemed to be an ocean. As his brain shifted from the void of delta into the deeply relaxed state of theta, he found that he could recognize the figures. They were dolphins, a mother and what seemed to be her infant. Sheeb floated just below them, watching the young mammal suckle at his mother's teat. Moonlight filtered in from the surface of the water, and Sheeb wondered how it was that he had been able to stay submerged for so long without going up for air.

"I'm dreaming! This is a dream," he thought. The thought itself began to bring him out of theta, and as his brain shifted into beta, he opened his eyes. It was still dark, though off on the horizon the sky had turned a light blue. Sheeb glanced over at the digital. It was 5 a.m. He had slept for three hours.

There was a knock at the door, and then the sound of it opening. It was Kathrina, wearing a purple bathrobe. She stood in the doorway smiling. Cast in the silver gray of early dawn, her image haunted him. Pulling back the covers, Sheeb let a pillow fall to the floor. Crossing the room soundlessly, Kathrina took off her robe and let it drop to the floor by the pillow.

Sitting on the bed beside him, she stroked his chest. Tracing the line of hair down to his belly, she bent over and lightly kissed his chest.

Kathrina continued to trace the line of hair, gently moving her hands downward into the rich musky dark jungle of his sex. She looked into his eyes, and then swung herself on top of him. Sheeb quivered with pleasure.

Sitting back on her haunches, Kathrina looked deep into Sheeb's eyes. Sheeb raised her fingers to his lips and kissed them. In the mirror on the far wall, he could see out the window above his head. Large puffs of pink and orange clouds were floating by in a turquoise sky. The same color as Kathrina's eyes, everywhere blue. Sheeb let himself sink back into the turquoise, the white linen, the smell and the feel of his lover.

The soft silence was broken by the squeal of Sheeb's portable phone. The built-in microprocessor had been programmed by Sheeb to receive all incoming calls, but to alert Sheeb only if the message was an emergency priority.

"Oh, come on!" Sheeb said pulling himself out of bed, "Give a guy a break!" Crossing the floor to the bureau, Sheeb lifted the cover to the cellphone. Looking briefly in the mirror, he saw Kathrina stretched out on the bed like a goddess guarding the window to a new world.

"Sheeb here."

"Sheeb... it's good to hear your voice again." It was Bach. His voice sounded weak, a raspy quality as if his vocal cords were becoming brittle. "The situation has deteriorated. I need to know your decision immediately. Do you want the job or not?"

Sheeb heard himself speak the word "Yes."

"Excellent. I'll need to see you in my office by noon tomorrow."

"All right." Sheeb hung up.

Turning around and walking back to the bed, Sheeb noticed that Kathrina was sitting upright in meditation. For a moment he just stood there looking past her to the far horizon where the sky was now turning a brilliant blue. Kathrina's eyes fluttered and opened. Looking straight into Sheeb, it seemed to him, in that moment, as if she were looking through him. Her voice sounded far away, as if borne into the room from some distant world. "Ran, " she said.

"What about him?" Sheeb asked.

"You have to go to him. I understand." She continued, her eyes unblinking. "He won't be on the earth plane much longer."

Sheeb felt his stomach sinking, and around him it seemed as if the furniture had suddenly started floating in the air once again. Speaking to the strange oracle sitting before him, Sheeb noticed that Kathrina's body was barely breathing. "What do you mean?" he asked.

"You know what I mean; you just won't let yourself know that you know. He won't be here in this Earth realm much longer. And it is good that you shall be with someone who was so close to you. It will be a great healing for the two of you."

CHAPTER TEN

Sheeb stood entranced, unable to move. Kathrina's arm hung motionless in the air, as if turned to marble, and then fell to her side. Slumping forward, she began to moan gently and after a few moments her breathing turned normal. Raising her head, she looked at Sheeb still standing in front of the bed. The luster in her eyes had returned, the vacant look of the last several minutes now gone.

"What was that?" Sheeb asked.

"Luna," Kathrina replied reluctantly. The dreaded moment had come.

Sheeb motioned for her to go on. Kathrina pulled a tassel of hair behind her ear. "Luna is a part of me; unfortunately she sometimes speaks when unasked. She sees from a place beyond time." There was a yearning in those last words that Sheeb couldn't miss.

Sheeb walked forward and sat at the foot of the bed. Outside the window, a lone seagull caught a glimmer of sunlight, its white underbelly a flash in the cerulean sky.

"She...?" Sheeb started to ask.

"Yes, she." Kathrina spoke softly. "Luna is a goddess."

"How does she know what will happen to Ran?"

Kathrina fingered the linen sheet at her feet, suddenly seeming unaccountably shy. "Luna possesses the power of omniscience. She has never been wrong, Sheeb."

There was anger in Sheeb's voice. "She said that Ran would die, damnit."

"I know."

Sheeb stood up and paced the room agitatedly. "Look, I think it's interesting, fascinating," Sheeb's hand cut the air like a knife, "that you can go into such deep altered states, but let's be clear about one thing. It's just an altered state. There is no goddess, not really. The gods and goddesses are creations, Kat, creations of our own minds."

"Then how do you explain what just happened?

"The human brain is capable of incredible things. Some part of you probably retrieved that information from my unconscious. It wouldn't have to go very deep, either." Sheeb turned and looked at her. "Look, we've only got six hours before I have to leave. I don't want to get into a discussion. Could we just drop the goddess thing for now?"

Kathrina nodded.

Sheeb walked over to the window and leaned on the ledge, looking out into the early morning light. Goddess or no goddess, he could feel the truth of her words. After all these years he would finally see Ran again only to lose him. Sheeb turned and leaned back against the window ledge. Staring at the floor, he followed a small speck of dust gently rising from the floor, lifted by invisible air currents. Perhaps Kat was right. Just because he didn't see Luna didn't automatically mean that she couldn't exist, but if she did...Sheeb did not want to imagine the implications. Taking a deep breath, he sighed.

"What's wrong?" Kathrina asked.

"Everything." There was hurt and frustration in his voice. Kathrina slipped out of bed and walked over to him. Taking his hands in hers, she searched his eyes. "I'm here, Sheeb."

"That's part of the problem, Kat. I want to be with you, and yet a part of me is already with Ran. You and I have so much to talk about. I've been looking forward to this time with you, but I have to leave in a few hours. So much is happening, my mind can't think straight. And if Luna is right, my best friend is going to die." Sheeb stared up at the ceiling, choking back tears.

Kathrina took his hand and motioned to the door. "I want to show you something." As they stepped into the early morning air, the sun emerged from behind a large puffy cloud and bathed them in warm golden light. Centauri followed close behind, sniffing the ground and wagging his tail eagerly.

All around them orchids were opening their mouths, drops of translucent nectar sparkling in the growing light. Off in the distance Sheeb could see the spire of the healing chamber pushing through the fronds of palm trees.

Kathrina walked slightly ahead, every now and then looking over her shoulder, a twinkle in her eye. Off to the side, Sheeb noticed Centauri marking one of the trees.

Rounding the bend to the healing chamber, Kathrina opened the door and motioned Sheeb inside. "Go ahead and get in. I've got to set the controls."

Stepping into the large circular pool, Sheeb watched Kathrina walk over to the command center.

Turning a series of switches, she set the processor on automatic and walked over to the pool. The most haunting music began to pour into the chamber. Sheeb had never in his life heard anything like it before. Broken fragments of resonant and beautiful sound floated through space, their primal frequencies vibrating every cell in Sheeb's body.

"What is this music?" he asked as he watched Kathrina lowering herself into the silky water.

"It's the sounds Shiva and Shakti make when they have sex. I recorded it and sent it through a Vocastrati."

"It's unbelievable," Sheeb said, the music growing stronger.

"Listen to me carefully. In a moment, the light crystal will be descending from the ceiling. When it does, you must stay connected with me. If you break away, you could be damaged. Whatever you do, whatever you experience, don't remove your hands from me. Do you understand?"

"Yes."

"Now take my hands like this." Kathrina clasped Sheeb's hands, positioning his fingers in such a way that their joined hands resembled a lotus floating in the air between them.

Suddenly the ceiling opened and an immense quartz crystal lowered itself into the room, light cascading everywhere from the flawless stone.

Kathrina looked into Sheeb's eyes. "Don't forget, keep hold of my hands."

Sheeb nodded.

At first it was a slight tingle at the top of his head. Swirls of energy began to move down into his face and neck, spreading into his hands. Then it turned to wildfire. In moments it had spread to every part of his body.

As the music grew in intensity the feelings became more pronounced. The fire thrust itself deeper into his flesh until it felt to him as if every cell were burning. The great crystal hummed as the rainbow of colors shifted to emerald green. Looking back at Kathrina standing across from him waist-deep in water, Sheeb had the impression that she had gone, and in her place, a priestess now stood before him. The impression lasted a moment, powerful despite its brevity.

Shiva and Shakti entered the tank through the underwater gate and began to circle them in long slow arcs. Kathrina's voice was strong. "Disregard them; they are drawn by the energy. Keep your eyes on me."

Looking into her eyes, Sheeb felt himself falling, falling into some kind of hole. It was as if his entire body was collapsing into a single point of light. Suddenly overcome with fear, he began to look around the pool, the point of light expanding.

Kathrina screamed at him. "My eyes! My eyes! Look into my eyes!"

Sheeb returned his gaze to hers, the point of light expanding as his body began to collapse once again. Filled with a terror he couldn't name, Sheeb realized that if he kept his gaze on her but held his energy back just behind the eyes so it did not meet hers, he could stop the sensation of his body collapsing in on itself.

Holding his energy in check, Sheeb watched Kathrina through narrowed eyes. In one moment she wore a crown on her head, in another Sheeb thought he saw a man standing beside her, enfolding her with large wings. Blinking his eyes, the visions disappeared, leaving Sheeb with the growing sense that the room was exploding into light. He could barely hear the dolphins circling them as the pulsations of energy grew stronger and stronger.

Suddenly Kathrina was gone. Sheeb tried to look around, but his head was locked into place. The room reverberated with a low hum as the dark hole reappeared. It pulled at him like a magnet, drawing him into itself. The vibrations grew stronger as Sheeb's body began to shake, every muscle in his body quivering. Sheeb screamed into the gaping mouth of nothingness. "No! I won't give in!"

Shivering and shaking from fatigue, Sheeb heard Kathrina's voice calling him. He felt a sudden pressure within the core of his brain, like something exploding. And then he saw her. Dressed in a white robe, she floated, suspended in the starlight night of space. Desperately, Sheeb reminded himself that they were not in interstellar space but in the healing chamber. And yet Kathrina continued to float in starlight.

"Oh, my god, she is in my mind!" Sheeb gasped.

Speaking to him from within his own mind, the image of Kathrina looked deep into his eyes. "Surrender, Sheeb," she coached. "Let go. You've got to let go of your body. If you don't, the light will tear you apart."

The light within the chamber swirled about him in a vortex, drawing him ever closer to the dark mouth of emptiness. Images streamed by like rapids. Without warning, Sheeb felt himself being hurled backward in time. Standing in the hallway at the orphanage, the young Sheeb watched as sunlight flooded in through the large window, filling the air with radiance. Hearing footsteps, the boy rubbed the tears from his eyes.

The doors to the hallway opened. "I mustn't show them how I feel," he thought. "I mustn't show them how I feel."

The words tumbled around him incessantly like some kind of mantra. The light swirled around him again. Lifting him from his feet, the light pulled him through the stone wall. The solidness of masonry gave way to the tumbling and terrifying rush of space.

He was spinning backward into a tunnel. Sheeb thought he heard angels singing, and then, a great darkness. Time stood still. It could have been hours or days. He could not tell.

Suddenly the darkness broke away and light flooded into his eyes. Looking down, he saw a baby being born. Without knowing how he knew, he knew the baby was him. The woman stretched out on the delivery table was his mother, and Sheeb saw clearly, for the first time, though he had always felt it somewhere, that she did not want him. And now, as his small life reached out for her, as his tiny mouth reached out for the teat that would bring precious liquid life, she turned and faced the wall.

Something powerful pulled him down into the body of the tiny child screaming in vain for its mother, screaming for a mother and for a comfort that would never come. It felt like terror, a metallic taste in the mouth. Sheeb felt something closing in around his tiny body. Something meant to be open and permeable was turning in on itself.

Sheeb, the man, felt the burning of tears in his throat as an anguished cry began to shake the air. Coughing and spitting, Sheeb's body spasmed with the awful pain. The scene of his birth slowly began to dissolve. In a panic he kicked and pawed the water, not quite clear where he was.

"It's okay," she said. "You're okay... just relax." Her voice was comforting. Taking a breath of air through his sobs of crying, Sheeb felt Kathrina pulling him close to her, pulling him to her like a newborn infant. Floating in her arms, Sheeb's head nuzzled up against her breasts. Stroking his hair, Kathrina kissed his face, every now and then wiping away his tears. In the soothing comfort of her presence, Sheeb was able to relax, the harsh memory of his birth now receding.

With a start, it occurred to Sheeb that the Vocastrati sounds had stopped some time ago. Catching a glimmer of light above him, he looked up to see the giant crystal disappearing behind hidden panels. All was silent again.

Stretching himself in the water, he pulled himself next to Kathrina. "What happened?" he asked. Kathrina ran her fingers through his wet hair. "The light," she stroked his cheek, "dissolved your separation."

"I thought it was going to rip me apart," Sheeb said.

"What you were feeling was not the light trying to destroy you, Sheeb." There was a sudden tenderness in her voice. "You were feeling your resistance to life." Sheeb wrapped his arms around his shoulders.

Kathrina continued. "We have memories... memories from this life, and I know you don't believe it," Kathrina's hand waved the air, "but from other lives as well. Pain and fear keep us trapped in separation. You experienced a deep fear from the moment of your birth, and you have been carrying it with you all these years. And like most of us, you have kept this fear in control by keeping love away, because love, my dear, confronts us where we hide the most...from ourselves. You've never really been able to let love in, Sheeb, because you were so terrified of feeling the pain you just experienced." Kathrina's hands went down to Sheeb's chest. "But now, where you had cut yourself off from the world, there is now an opening."

Sheeb looked up at her.

"Through that opening, you can now replace the fear."

"Replace it with what?" Sheeb asked.

Kathrina looked deeply into his eyes before speaking. "Love, Sheeb... just love."

There was a burning of tears in the back of his throat again. Sheeb reached over and pulled her close. Feeling her body next to him sent pleasure through every cell of his body. The smell of her hair was intoxicating.

"Kat?"

"Yes."

"I want to make love."

"Now?" Kathrina asked in mock surprise as her hand slid down his inner thigh.

"And I don't know why, "Sheeb continued, "but I want to do it in the Sphere."

"Underwater?" she asked.

Sheeb nodded.

"How exciting!" Kathrina walked over to the steps that led from the tank. Reaching for a towel, she looked back at Sheeb with a nymph-like grin. She nodded towards the door. "After you, Captain Nemo."

CHAPTER ELEVEN

Kathrina led Sheeb down a seldom-used path. The small dirt trail twisted back on itself, drawing a thin line through thick foliage and thousands of blooming hybrid orchids. Their upturned cups glistened with nectar and the heady perfume intoxicated Sheeb as he followed Kathrina, admiring how the muscles of her long slender back fed into the firm roundness of her buttocks.

There was a rustle in the trees to the right, Centauri chasing a small animal through the undergrowth. Tuning in to the canine, Sheeb's mind was flooded with the scent of moist humus. The faint sweetly acrid smell of exposed roots wafted in the air. A few inches away, a rodent was anxiously burrowing into its den.

Sheeb's communion with Centauri ended abruptly as he bumped into Kathrina, who had stopped. Feeling her soft flesh against his body, Sheeb slid his arms around her waist. "Sorry."

Kathrina turned back and gave him a kiss. "Here we are."

The path had opened to the small lagoon where Sheeb had anchored the hydrojet. "This would be a good place to drop the Sphere," Kathrina announced. "The water is deep and clear."

"Great!"

Sheeb ran over to the floating dock and entered the hydrojet. He set the controls on automatic and the rear end of the vessel slid open. Sheeb motioned Kathrina into the Sphere as he checked the oxygen and battery levels.

Satisfied, Sheeb punched in the launch instructions, the bay motors humming as the large plastishield Sphere was lowered gently into the water.

As the submerge tanks flooded, the clear bubble began to sink beneath the surface of the water. The bright light of day turned blue as the Sphere sank deeper and deeper into the waters of the lagoon.

The bright colors of genetically engineered Torino fish darted back and forth as the Sphere invaded their domain. The incandescent yellows of the female's underbellies signaled their readiness for mating. Dots of rouge pink speckled their yellow abdomens. And the males, their backs a deep cobalt blue, swam around the females in a show of underwater pyrotechnics.

As the Sphere dropped deeper and deeper into the lagoon, Sheeb watched a bed of hydras swaying in the unseen ocean currents. Kathrina slid her hands around his waist, pulling him close to her. Nibbling his ear, she pointed out the mouth to a large cave. "In there.... take us in there," she said.

"What is it?" Sheeb asked.

"It's an underwater cavern. It opens up into a large chamber that rises into the mountain. There's a clearing above the waterline." Kathrina's hand slid up and caressed Sheeb's chest.

Sheeb turned to look at her.

Kathrina grinned like a water sprite. "You'll love it!"

Sheeb turned the Sphere toward the dark mouth of the cave. As they entered the shadow of the entrance, a large manatee slid gracefully beside them, its dark tail silently slicing the water.

The light blue of the lagoon turned gray and then black as Sheeb guided the Sphere deeper into the throat of the cave. Turning on the Sphere's flood lights, he watched as the floor of the cave began to rise. The channel shot abruptly upward toward an even greater darkness, the only sound that of the Sphere's motors. The walls of the cave, ever closing in on them, glistened a rosy pink in the incandescent light of the flood lamps.

As the Sphere rounded a large boulder, Kathrina reached over and flipped off the floodlights. For a moment it seemed that they were in utter darkness, but then Sheeb's eyes adjusted. There was the faintest glow filtering down from above. Looking upward, Sheeb noticed that they were nearing the surface of the water, and as the Sphere broke the surface, Sheeb leaned back into Kathrina's breasts and sighed.

Guiding the vehicle over to a low rise of sand and rock, Sheeb let the vessel ground itself against the shore. Opening the hatch, the two of them stepped out onto the soft sand.

The air was moist and warm. The inside of the cave stretched outward all around them like a gigantic womb. Phosphorescent stalactites hung from the vast ceiling.

Kathrina took his hand and led him up to a ledge.

"How did you find this?" Sheeb asked.

"Luna showed it to me in a vision."

"Maybe there's more to this Luna thing than I thought," Sheeb said.

"She said that this is a sacred chamber. It has an incredible energy. Can you feel it?"

"I feel...something." Sheeb smiled inwardly, since the feeling he mentioned was the feeling of his cock swelling with excitement. Kathrina looked more beautiful than he had ever seen her before. Bathed in the warm pink light of the moist chamber, her soft skin radiated, calling him to her like the moon must call sea turtles from the sea to their matings.

Looking at her standing there, Kathrina seemed to be radiating a soft white light. His sex ached with the rush of salt blood. He wanted her. As he crossed toward her, Kathrina turned to see the burning of his passion. A breath of air pushed itself past her open lips. Sheeb's hand reached out for her; she touched his open fingers like a hydra reaching out into a milky sea. As Sheeb's body pressed against her, Kathrina's nipples grew hard, and feeling them against his flesh, Sheeb bent over to kiss them. Kathrina arched her back in pleasure as Sheeb kissed her heart and throat and chin, and finally the deep moistness of her mouth. His hands rose into the air and caressed her hair as her tongue quivered in the damp heat of his mouth. They stood swaying in the currents of their entwining as pheromones of passion filled the air, intoxicating them.

Sheeb gently lowered Kathrina onto the silk-like sand at their feet and wrapped his legs around her. As he pressed his body against hers, a quiver of pleasure-electricity pulsed through his loins and looking deeply into Kathrina's eyes, he smiled. His eyes looked past her for a moment to see the placid surface of the water. Their reflections had been captured in the watery mirror, and Sheeb luxuriated in the beauty of their bodies and in the grace of their intertwining. The illusion was complete—as if cast in marble, they could have easily been lovers carved centuries before.

Something stirred in the water, perhaps a fish. The mirror-like surface of the water was marred, and the rhythm of the tiny waves lulled Sheeb into a momentary trance. He closed his eyes, and a vision passed through his mind. The floor of the sea had dropped away into a deep grotto, and he was standing before an ancient archway. On the other side of the hewn stone, Sheeb could see strange ovoids strewn along the floor, their odd shapes reminding him of eggs. About a hundred yards away, Sheeb could see a large pearl resting on a marble altar. It lay open to the water, and was radiating a soft, milky light.

Opening his eyes, he gazed at the face in front of him, the deep turquoise blue of her irises enfolding him. Sheeb raised a hand to her face and gently caressed her cheek, looking deeper into her eyes. Something was happening: Kathrina was leaving; Luna was taking her place. He could sense it. Quickly dropping into sync, Sheeb followed her... followed her into the underwater temple, where the goddess had already stepped out of the luminescent pearl. The goddess looked at him as a raptor must look at its prey.

Sensing that he was in some kind of danger, Sheeb decided to step into her world anyway. There was something he had to know. As he walked through the underwater grotto, compelling energies emanated from the ovoids, trying to lull him into a deep sleep. He instinctively looked into Luna's eyes, and as long as he looked into the infinite pool of her pupils, the tiredness from the ovoids could not touch him. But the price of looking into the blue of her eyes was a burning that spread throughout his entire body.

Approaching the seven stone steps that led to the altar, Sheeb's legs felt like they might give out from under him, for the goddess had suddenly grown a hundred arms. And in her multitudinous hands she brandished a collection of daggers, swords, and tridents, each of them trembling with a fierce power.

A lone manatee swam between them as time seemed suddenly to stand still. Looking upward, Sheeb could barely see the light of the sun filtering down through the crystal-clear water. For a moment he marveled at the depth he had wandered into.

"There are different laws down here than on the surface." The goddess spoke, one of her many arms swaying in the water. "You'd best learn them if you wish to survive."

"What do you mean?"

"You found me through chance, and it is only through your contact with Kathrina that you are here. But even though you managed to stumble onto this place, you are incapable of understanding the significance of this grotto or its implications."

"How can you be so sure?" Sheeb asked.

The goddess waived one of her tridents. "It is obvious."

"What's obvious?" Sheeb asked, annoyed.

The goddess looked straight into his eyes. "It is clear that you are blinded by your intellectual arrogance."

"That may be true, I don't know. But I know that I love Kathrina, and if you are a part of her, I want to understand you."

Luna laughed. "Understand? First of all, I am not a part of Kathrina, she is a part of me. Secondly, understanding me is beyond your capacity. As for your love," the goddess waved one of her tridents through the air, "your love is very limited. Your love cannot bear what Kathrina must become." The goddess planted the trident on the ocean floor, a floor that was littered with oyster shells.

Her eyes bore into Sheeb with an awful power. "I am preparing Kathrina for a new world, and your love is inadequate. Your love is, quite frankly, a hindrance."

"Then what must I do to make my love worthy?" Sheeb demanded.

Luna looked at him askance. "You have no idea what you are asking."

"Then tell me."

Luna arched her eyebrows as one of her arms raised a scythe. "Do you see this?" she bellowed.

"Yes," Sheeb replied.

"This is what is required for your human love." Luna shook her razor-sharp scythe with such a force, the waters around her trembled. "If you can bear it, and most humans can't," she added, "your mortal love must be pruned like dead limbs are pruned from a tree. The scythe in my hands must cut through your fears of loss, for as you stand before me, your love is a counterfeit. What you mistake for love is nothing more than fear disguised. Your fears of abandonment keep you tethered to Kathrina, but this is not the love of which I speak." Luna took a deep breath and sighed. "If you are capable of bearing the loss of who you are, then and only then will you understand."

"Then so be it!" yelled Sheeb, his eyes filled with tears.

The goddess held her silence for what seemed like aeons, and then she waved him toward the entrance to the grotto. Her words were soft and tender.

"By the power of your words may this come to pass, but for now you'd best leave. The ovoids are starting to drain your strength."

She was right. Sheeb could feel his energy ebbing away. He walked toward the arch, but then stopped, and turning, he faced Luna, his heart suddenly filled with an inexplicable sense of love and reverence. Her words, though harsh and seemingly cruel, were honest. He was grateful for the truth, even if it had wounded his pride. He bowed before the mysterious goddess and said, "Thank you."

Luna arched an eyebrow and smiled as if pleasantly surprised. One of her hands rose in the water and a beam of whitish light poured from one of her open palms into Sheeb's heart. Filled with a peace and a calm he had never known before, Sheeb left the grotto. Outside the archway, Shakti was waiting. Mounting her, Sheeb rode the dolphin to the surface, the grotto quickly giving way to the bright blue of the surface.

As he opened his eyes, Sheeb saw Kathrina looking back at him smiling.

"Welcome back." Her words were soft, her kiss warm and moist.

Hearing the familiar clicks and whistles of the Precious Ones, Sheeb looked around to see Shiva and Shakti swimming in the water of the cave. Sheeb raised a hand to his head. "I don't believe it."

"Believe it," Kathrina said.

Sheeb rolled onto his side so that he was facing her. Kathrina looked back at him, her fingers brushing the slight line of hair that ran from his chest to his belly.

"Kat?"

"Yes, Sheeb?" Kathrina's eyes reflected Sheeb's image back to himself.

"What did Luna mean when she said that she was preparing you?"

CHAPTER TWELVE

Kathrina turned and sat up. For the longest time she didn't speak, only her left hand tracing small circles in the sand. She knew she must tell him, but how? How could he, would he ever understand? Kathrina felt a tear come to her eyes as a deep sadness washed over her, the irony tasting bitter in her mouth.

God, how Luna had filled her! Her heart sometimes ached from the fullness of holding every creature on the planet. That feeling, that knowing, how could she ever describe it to Sheeb? No words could ever convey it.

Only days before, she had found a small bird washed up onto the beach. Picking the fragile creature up in her hands, Kathrina had felt the pulling. In her mind, she felt herself floating upward. Soaring above the water's edge, in the freedom of her mind, she looked down into the blue-green water beneath her. Whitecaps glistened in the sun, and in the quiet lakes between the waves, schools of fish swam in torrents. Kathrina had felt herself falling to her knees weeping, weeping for all of life's yearning. Through the power of her vision she could look down from the skies to see herself standing on the beach, the white sands reaching into the clear water, and farther out, tides of fish were swimming eastward toward their feeding grounds. In that brief moment, she had known the deepest and most primal feelings of all life on the planet. Swooning from the enormity of her sudden perception, Kathrina had heard Luna speak to her. "You are still just on the surface of things." A moment of silence, and then the goddess was gone.

Kathrina felt Sheeb pressing his hand against her thigh.

"What's wrong?" he asked.

Kathrina turned and looked into his eyes. "I can't put in into words, Sheeb, at least words that you would understand."

"Then show me what you want me to know."

Slightly taken aback, Kathrina smiled and raked a hand through her hair. "Okay, but I want to show you in the Sphere."

Sheeb got up and walked silently to the waiting plastishield. Slipping in beside him, Kathrina pressed her cheek against his shoulder as Sheeb lowered the hatch and began to submerge the bubble. The radiant light of the chamber dimmed as the Sphere sank deeper and deeper into the dark throat of the cave.

As they descended toward the entrance, Sheeb noted that Kathrina sat pressed against the shield, looking out fixedly into the dim light. It was only after they had passed from the lip of the entrance into the turquoise blue of the lagoon that she turned and looked at him.

Setting the controls on automatic, Sheeb leaned back in his seat and put his arms behind his head. The Sphere would now rise in a slow ascent toward the surface. Moments later, the two dolphins emerged, kicking their powerful tails. Gliding up beside the Sphere, Shiva and Shakti cavorted and nosed each other, seemingly oblivious of the two humans inside the floating plastishield.

Kathrina pressed her fingers against the bubble as if to touch the playing dolphins. Sighing, she turned to Sheeb. "Are you sure you want to know?" she asked.

Sheeb felt his throat swallow. "Yes."

"Then look into my eye, just my left eye."

As he gazed into the deep turquoise of her eye, Sheeb felt something inside of him turning. The Sphere was filling with colors and little dots of dancing light. In a flash, everything was gone—no Kathrina, no bubble, just white light. A strange yet comforting calmness overtook him as he drifted deeper and deeper into the strange apparition.

From a passageway in the middle of the light, a lone woman approached him carrying a large white pearl. Opening the iridescence, she motioned Sheeb to look inside. A kaleidoscope of images cascaded through him: an old woman dying alone on a hilltop, her clothes tattered and flapping in the cold wind; children playing hopscotch; a foal being born in the midst of daisies; birds flying homeward through dark autumn skies.

"How can this be?" he thought. And still the images continued flowing through him like some vast river. Honeybees crawled into the throats of flowers, their heady perfume thick in the air, while elephants kicked up storms of dust on the plains of the Serengeti. Sheeb felt his heart aching from the power of so much life. Everywhere he looked, life reached out to him, calling him, beseeching him. For in every eye of every animal, from the tiniest prairie squirrels to the mammoth whales, he saw an unspoken question. And yet somewhere, deep inside of himself, Sheeb knew that he must not recognize their pleading, which was his own pleading, for to do so would rip something away, something he had carefully wrapped around himself a long time ago. To take the self-made shroud away would leave him utterly naked, without anything to keep the illusion in place. And he needed the illusion. He needed to believe that he was separate from the world.

With sheer power of will, Sheeb forced himself back into normal awareness. The light faded, and before his eyes, Kathrina sat looking back at him. The sweet odor of her hair filled the air, reminding him of the smell of flowers he had sensed during the apparition. He finally knew what the goddess had meant. Was it really possible for one human life to hold within its burgeoning heart all life on the planet? The thought boggled him.

"You know," Sheeb said, his eyes tracking a few dots of light that still hovered in the Sphere, "I didn't think it was possible, but I love you even more."

"In what way?" Kathrina's words sounded nonchalant, though the back of her throat was burning.

"I didn't know it was possible to love the way you do. I..." Sheeb's words trailed off as he looked at the tears rolling silently down Kathrina's cheeks.

Kathrina wiped the tears away, her words sounding oddly childlike. "I was afraid you'd leave me when you saw that. I was afraid it would scare you." Her hands shaped a peculiar geometry through the air, "and drive you away."

CHAPTER THIRTEEN

Alex Vollen leaned back in his chair, his hands tucked behind his head. Staring past the letters on the screen before him, he searched the luminous screen of the terminal, as if he might somehow fathom the meaning behind the words, might somehow recognize the deeper message hidden within the architecture of sound and symbol.

Behind him lying on the bed, his luggage waited. Within hours he would be in Bethesda. By tomorrow he would meet Sheeb, the man who brought more questions than answers. And the biggest question of all lay still unanswered, somewhere in that light behind the words that floated before Vollen's eyes.

RAN FARR STILL IN CATATON-IC STATE. SHEEB PROCEEDING TO RENDEZVOUS POINT AS SCHEDULED. PLEASE ACKNOWLEDGE RECEIPT OF TRANSMIS-SION. FUGUE ONE OUT.

Vollen punched in his response with one hand while the other massaged the taut muscles of his neck.

ACKNOWLEDGED. RUNNER OUT.

CHAPTER FOURTEEN

Hours had passed, and the first signs of dawn were streaking across the sky as Sheeb walked along the beach alone. The light blue pastels of the horizon gave way to rosy pinks and light magentas as the Earth rotated toward the sun. Sheeb had left Kathrina sleeping, her hands folded beneath her head like a small child.

Walking now among seabirds diving and wading for food, Sheeb looked out to the far horizon. Soon he would be leaving—too soon. Not since his times with Ran, had Sheeb opened so deeply to another person. Gazing down at his feet, Sheeb watched hundreds of little crabs scurrying in every direction as the tide washed in, threatening to pull the tiny creatures into the depths. Sheeb sighed and kept walking, his eyes now scanning the dark horizon. Dark clouds were rolling in, and hanging low on the horizon, they muted the exquisite colors of dawn into mottled shades of gray.

Back at the cottage, Sheeb looked in on Kathrina. There was no one in the bedroom, only the white bed linens reflecting the light of dawn through the open window. Sauntering into the kitchen, he found her making toast. Motioning Sheeb to sit, she carried over a small plate of sliced Equa fruit and set it on the table.

A hybird of genetic engineering, the Equa had become very popular in its ten-year existence. Gourmands the world over clamored for its rich and luscious flesh. The Equa could demand any price, and its creator, botanist Louis d'Moraux, was a reputed billionaire as a result of his creation.

Slipping a piece of the fruit into his mouth, Sheeb sniffed the aromatic perfume that suddenly filled the air, a combination of honeysuckle and melon. Centauri entered the kitchen and padded over to Sheeb, sitting down beside him, and resting his head on his lap. Sheeb's fingers scratched the dog's ears as Kathrina returned to the table bearing toast and chamomile tea. They didn't speak much, mostly communing in long valleys of silence.

Later, standing on the float by the hydrojet, Sheeb kissed Kathrina goodbye as seabirds circled overhead. Centauri had already entered and found a place for himself beside the pilot's chair in front of the control panel.

Kathrina kissed him tenderly on the mouth, and wished him well. Sheeb pulled her in close. Feeling the contour of her back, his hands yearned to hold her forever. But time, inexorably moving onward, pulled at him like an outgoing tide. Breaking their embrace, Sheeb said goodbye. Kathrina smiled and brushed his cheek. Turning toward the path, she walked away without looking back.

Sheeb closed the hatch behind him, and made his way to his station and Centauri. After buckling himself in, he throttled the hydrojet forward away from the dock and into the gray light of morning. Clearing the coral reef, Sheeb throttled the Mercury full forward, and the hydrojet sliced through the air like a scythe over water.

Out in the open, Sheeb set the hydrojet on autopilot and sat back in his seat, interlacing his fingers behind his head. Every now and then the sun would burst through the bank of gray clouds setting the surface of the ocean sparkling with light.

Sheeb could feel Centauri pulling at him. The dog sat perfectly still, his tail gently wagging, but his mind was searching Sheeb, searching for what troubled him. Like an old friend, the animal beseeched him, asking without words, "What's wrong?"

Sheeb's hand fell gently to Centauri's head. Rubbing the back of the animal's skull, Sheeb thought about what awaited him. How would Ran look after all these years? What was this Mind War Machine, and how had Ran become involved? It wasn't the kind of thing that would have interested the Ran he had known in college. But perhaps most disturbing of all was the question of the cube. How would he retrieve it from wherever it had been sent? And could he recapture it in time?

CHAPTER FIFTEEN

Alex Vollen stepped back against the handrail as a nondescript person crowded the elevator. When they reached the third floor, two secretaries bearing video laser discs departed for their respective offices. A company rep of some sort got off at the twelfth, leaving Vollen alone with a delivery boy and someone resembling the Alan Sheeb he had seen in the dossier pictures.

At the twenty-third floor the boy pushed his cart of snacks toward the opening doors. Vollen watched as the assortment of bubble waters, sodas, sandwiches, apples, and imitation Equa fruit rolled out the door. From the rear, Vollen noticed something about the boy that he hadn't seen before. Running from the nape of his neck down to his collar were two parallel scars. The boy was obviously a member of the Rashtans.

Drawn from street kids, runaways, ecstasy addicts, and university dropouts, the Rashtans were reputedly amoral.

Although varied in their politics, all Rashtans had something in common—the ritual of initiation. Exactly what happened to them as they entered the cult was shrouded in utmost secrecy, but every Rashtan emerged with two continuous parallel scars that ran down from their neck to their ass, to their genitals and up their belly to their heart.

Vollen had heard of them before, but he had never actually seen one. He had to control a desire to throw the kid against the wall and strip him. Did the scars really go all the way around the boy's body?

The door closed, bringing Vollen back from his fantasy. Sheeb had moved closer to the door, oblivious of his fellow passenger. Leaning back against the wall, he watched Sheeb for a few moments as the elevator climbed soundlessly to the thirty-third floor. Vollen found his anonymity enticing and he relished it. The pictures in the files had been face shots only; now he could appraise the rest of him—strong thighs and a fairly muscular body. Vollen could tell that Sheeb sensed him scrutinizing him. He nodded politely when Sheeb turned around, but said nothing. Sheeb turned back and faced the doors.

When the elevator came to a stop at Bach's penthouse office, Sheeb stepped quickly into the hallway. Vollen followed several feet behind. As the two of them approached the receptionist, the young blonde looked up and smiled at Vollen.

"How was your vacation, Margo?" Vollen asked with a twinkle in his eye.

"Too short." Margo fiddled with her pen and grinned. "Bach is waiting for you, Alex." Turning to Sheeb, she asked, "Can I help you?"

"Margo, this is Alan Sheeb. He'll be joining us."

The receptionist looked down at her appointment book and nodded.

Sheeb was stunned. Vollen

motioned to the door. "I'll explain later," he said in a hushed whisper.

Sheeb nodded and followed him into Bach's massive office. The two men stepped onto the burgundy carpet and started the long walk through history that meandered toward Alfred Bach's desk. Sheeb could see him on the far side of the room with an attendant dressed in white. Bach was sitting in a wheelchair.

Vollen had walked on ahead of him, briefly stopping at the fossilized remains of a she-wolf from the Ice Age. Sheeb's eyes were again kidnapped by the exploding cobalt skies of El Greco. Both men paused at the mummified boy from Pompeii, and for a moment their eyes met.

"Gentlemen, please. I haven't got all day." Bach's raspy voice echoed from across the room. The deterioration of his body was affecting his vocal cords.

Vollen and Sheeb walked the several yards to Bach and his silent attendant. "Excuse me for not rising to greet you, but I am very weak." Bach motioned to the couch like an impresario. "Please be seated."

"Well, Sheeb," he continued, "I assume you've met Alex."

"Not really. We just came up on the elevator together."

"I see." Bach took a small cup of liquid from the young man at his side. "Alex Vollen is the security officer for this project and you are to report anything you uncover directly to him. He has just returned from Austria and he will be stationed with you at the facility. In fact," Bach took a sip and handed the empty cup back to the male nurse, "he will be escorting you there in one of our alpha shuttles."

"Alex," Bach motioned for Vollen to take over.

Vollen rose from the couch and retrieved a folder sitting atop the desk. Crossing the sitting area and handing it to Sheeb, he sat in one of the opposite chairs.

"What do you know about the Mind War Machine?" Vollen asked Sheeb.

"Not much...just what Alfred told me. It's some kind of microprocessor that interfaces with the psychic abilities of a human operator, isn't it?"

Vollen nodded.

"The technicalities weren't explained, but I believe it's supposed to be able to send objects from this dimension into another. I believe they call it translating."

"Correct." Vollen raised a hand to his chin resting it there. "And what do you know about Ran Farr?"

Sheeb glanced at Bach, and then back at Vollen. "I don't know what you mean. We were room-mates back in college, as you undoubtedly know."

"Undoubtedly."

"What is it that you specifically want to know?" Sheeb asked.

"I am referring to the fact that he disappeared ten years ago. Are you aware of what he did in those ten years?"

"No," Sheeb replied curtly.

"Uhmm...." Vollen rubbed his chin. "You will, I suspect, find this dossier very interesting." Vollen handed Sheeb a folder.

Sheeb stroked the front of the binder as he spoke. "Ran was a... very interesting person."

"I'm sure he still is. My concern, as you can appreciate, is not with the man himself, but with the information that he has inside his brain." Vollen continued. "Ran did not keep notes. Every aspect of the MWM is in his head. As Mr. Bach has, no doubt, informed you, Ran has not spoken for several weeks." Vollen arose from his chair and walked over to the Amoretzi, turning to face Sheeb. "Ran spends all his time in the estate greenhouse looking at orchids."

"That's it? He doesn't do anything else?" Sheeb asked.

"Pretty much. He just sits and looks at the flowers with some kind of grin on his face. He doesn't speak, and he hasn't eaten since the incident."

"What incident?"

"A moment before Ran successfully translated the cube, a number of people in the laboratory heard a loud hum, which they described as a kind of weird insect-like sound."

"That's strange," Sheeb offered. "How do you account for it?"

"I don't," Vollen replied. "And that's not the strangest part of it, either. About half of the team also saw a purplish light around the cube just before it disappeared. But the in-house video cameras and the recording equipment did not pick up the reported sound or the weird light. It did record Ran saying 'I have an odd feeling' right after the cube was translated. When the assistants asked him what he meant, he said nothing."

Vollen walked back to his chair, obviously moved by what he was about to say. "Later that afternoon the staff found him naked, hugging one of the electrician's dogs. He kept asking the dog to forgive him."

"For what?" Sheeb asked perplexed.

Vollen shrugged his shoulders. "No one knows. And from that moment Ran hasn't said a word. It's as if he is lost in some kind of other world."

"I'm curious about something," Sheeb said.

"Yes?" Vollen asked.

"Why do you call sending the cube into another dimension 'translating'?"

"Ran came up with the term, and it simply became part of the project's jargon."

"Odd," Sheeb mumbled to himself.

"How so?" Vollen asked.

"It's just that the word 'translation' is a linguistic term. I would think that Ran would have used a term borrowed from theoretical physics. The only plausible reason I can think of for using a linguistically-based word is that Ran must have thought that he was dealing with language. I just don't get it."

"Gentlemen," Bach broke into the conversation. "Back to the task at hand, please."

Bach turned his wheelchair to face Sheeb. "Your job is to find out exactly what happened, and to retrieve the cube as soon as possible. After you have the cube in your possession, we will shut down the project and destroy all the records."

The attendant rolled up Bach's shirt sleeve as he spoke. Placing a hypodermic in his arm, the nurse injected a small ampule into the financier's vein. Bach winced and took a deep breath. "We haven't got much time. As soon as you discover anything, give the information to Vollen and no one else. Is that understood?"

"Yes."

"Good." Bach turned his attention to Vollen and began to ask him questions about logistics. As the two of them discussed security, Sheeb shifted his brain into alpha and dropped into sync with Vollen. The man mystified him. Swimming into the sea of neurological synapses, Sheeb could sense the strength of the man. There was something driving Vollen, but he couldn't identify it. Vollen had obviously mastered the art of mind suspension. The energy surrounding the secret or secrets—it was impossible to tell if there was more than one, was relentless.

Vollen could sense Sheeb searching his mind. Turning, Vollen looked at his would-be trapper. His face was quiescent; only the slight dilation of his pupils revealed his awareness of Sheeb's covert activity. But within Vollen's sea of holoimages, Sheeb suddenly found himself face to face with a large wolf. Just an instant before, Sheeb had been tracking Vollen through the security officer's mind, which had presented itself as a dark forest. Rounding an imaginary boulder, Sheeb had stumbled upon the wolf. Their eyes met and the shock brought Sheeb out of sync. He was back in the room, and he looked up to see Vollen staring at him. It was the oddest impression—from behind Vollen's eyes, the wolf was looking intently at Sheeb. Vollen looked at him for only an instant and then turned back to his conversation with Bach.

"So that settles it," Bach said. "I would like to speak with Sheeb alone for a few moments. After that the two of you can leave for the estate."

"Yes, sir." Vollen rose from his chair.

"You can wait outside at the receptionist." Bach motioned toward the outer office.

Vollen nodded, and started down the corridor of relics towards the door. Bach motioned the attendant to follow him. "If I need you, I'll buzz."

Sheeb watched Vollen as he walked briskly through Bach's corridor of history. Pausing briefly at the fossilized wolf, his hand gently, almost imperceptibly, touched the Plexiglas case and then dropped to his side. Closing the door soundlessly behind them, Vollen and the attendant left Bach alone with Sheeb.

Sheeb broke the silence. "How long have you known Vollen?"

"Three years, why?"

"He's hiding something."

Bach smiled. "Were you tracking him?"

"Yes."

"I suspect that Vollen has many secrets. He is one of the top information security people in the world." Bach's finger touched the computer controls for the wheelchair. Rolling closer to Sheeb, still sitting on the couch, Bach waved his hand in the air. "Let him have his secrets. Every man has some, at least one, and if we're lucky we have several."

Sheeb laughed.

"Besides, I don't feel that Vollen's secret is any threat to the project, and right now that's all that matters."

"As you wish."

Bach grunted. "Would you mind pouring me a glass of wine?"

"Not at all." Sheeb rose from the couch and walked towards the bar.

"Open the Chateau Margaux. Help yourself, if you care to." Bach turned his chair around to face the large window. The light of late afternoon had dimmed to a golden glow. The brass sculpture of St. Michael slaying the dragon sparkled with the reflected rays of sunbeam.

Sheeb returned with two filled glasses. Bach took his with an unsteady hand. "So..." Bach raised his glass to his lips. "How was your visit?"

"Too short."

There was a long silence as Bach stared out the large window as if searching for something. He finally spoke, still staring off into space. "Do you love her?"

The question surprised Sheeb. "Yes, Alfred, I do."

"And does she love you?"

"Very much."

Bach turned and looked straight into Sheeb's eyes. "That's all that matters, Sheeb. Love is the only thing that matters."

"I don't understand."

Bach laughed. "You will, you will." He turned back to the window and the setting sun. "What I mean to say is, after everything is done, after having built this empire, after living longer than ever dreamed possible...after having beaten back the starkiller, if only temporarily, there is only one thing that truly matters to me, and that is my Heleina...my Heleina who is no more...who has been gone for over a century now, yet is still alive in my mind." Bach raised a hand to his forehead and rubbed it.

Sheeb took a sip from his glass and sat in one of the chairs opposite Bach. "Alfred, if Heleina's love is all that matters to you, why are you dealing with this Mind War thing, especially now?"

"Because I understand history, Sheeb. The Mind War Machine should never have been created, and since I am in the position to destroy this monstrosity before it poisons human destiny, it is my ethical duty to do so."

Bach touched the computer controls and wheeled himself around. Motioning Sheeb to follow him, he rolled down the corridor of relics to a small Plexiglas case. His shaking hand rose in the air and pointed to the charred bones of a small boy. "Hiroshima...this unfortunate lad happened to be on his way to school when the U.S. government dropped the world's first atomic bomb. Like all humans thrown into that darkness of death, there's not much left." Bach took a deep breath, as if struck by an intense irony. "This small boy's legacy was to be killed by an advanced technology that was to shatter not only his life, but the rest of human history as well."

Bach continued, seemingly oblivious to his listener. "That act of fission split the atomic force, a force that had been meant to hold things together, not blow them apart." Bach turned around and faced Sheeb, his eyes boring into him. "The Mind War Machine makes the atomic bomb look like child's play. Its potential to alter human history even overshadows the nightmare of Hiroshima and Nagasaki. And I will not," Bach's shaking fist hit the armrest of his wheelchair, "let it fall into the hands of self-glorified monkeys."

Sheeb took a deep breath, his respect for Bach deepening. The financier reached out and touched Sheeb's arm. "I want you to know something. I chose you for this job because you were the best person available, purely a rational decision. However..." Bach stared out the window again. "From the first day I met you in my office, I knew that given another time, another circumstance, we might have become friends." A single tear glistened in Bach's eye.

Sheeb started to raise his hand to touch Bach, but he rolled his wheelchair closer to the large window, stopping a few feet from the large vista. For the longest time, Bach just sat there watching the setting sun as the sky turned into mauves and red orange. "It's funny, but for the first time in my life I realize that I may not be immortal. Imagine that!" Bach turned and looked at Sheeb. "I was so sure that I could beat death."

Sheeb started to speak, but Bach silenced him with an upraised hand. "Don't say anything. Just stay here with me for a few more minutes."

Sheeb nodded. Standing in the dying light of sunset, Sheeb gently placed a hand on Bach's shoulder. Bach turned to him and smiled. The two men watched the blazing sky in silence. As Bethesda rotated further away from the sun, the sky exploded into molten gold. Time stood still for one glorious moment. And then the red-tinged clouds overhead seemed to cool, their fire slowly fading like dying embers.

The two silent figures were transfixed by the awesome movement of light and darkness, neither noticing the passage of time. Bach finally dismissed Sheeb. "Vollen's waiting...don't forget what I said."

"I won't."

"Good." Bach waved him off. "On your way out, tell my nurse to come back in."

"Yes."

Walking through the corridor of relics, Sheeb felt a heaviness. The burning quasar of Alfred

Bach was dying, and there wasn't anything anyone could do to stop it. As he reached the door, Sheeb heard Bach laughing. It was an odd and powerful laugh, a sound he had not heard before. Turning, he looked back. The old man's eyes were on fire, reflecting the very last dying glimmer of the setting sun.

CHAPTER SIXTEEN

Alpha Lyra rocketed through the last tenuous layers of the atmosphere as the shuttle bearing Vollen, Sheeb, and Centauri leveled into low Earth orbit. Beneath them the planet rolled itself over into the ever-present solar stream, that hurling river of light from Earth's burning star. Below, white clouds drifted off the coast of Sri Lanka. Minutes later, the Earth passed into the edge of night and the small vessel was thrown into darkness as it passed over India.

Sheeb looked down at the sparkle of lights. New Delhi lay spread out beneath them like an ancient carpet. As they passed deeper into the darkness of Earth's night, Sheeb could make out stars radiating their primeval light into the awesomeness of space.

There was Sirius, the dog star. Its light, now millions of years old, had left the star's surface of burning hydrogen when fish first breathed air on Earth's fledgling surface. That ancient light was just now reaching the planet.

Sheeb glanced back to check on Centauri strapped into one of the crew chairs. He seemed contented enough. Turning his attention back to the panel of instruments, Sheeb watched Vollen making fine adjustments to the on-board computer, the array of lights before them on the control panel reminding Sheeb of the lights from New Delhi now a thousand miles behind them.

Spotting one of the toggle switches labeled R.A.N., Sheeb pointed. "What is that?"

"Radial Axis Neutralizer...it stops the craft from spinning, should the computer fail," noted Vollen.

Sheeb nodded and looked out the window to the sea of stars. His thoughts turned to Ran. The dossier had revealed someone he had never known. Had the Ran of his memory been mostly illusion, or had the man changed? Sheeb searched the canopy of stars as if looking for an answer. Off to the right, the Big Dipper lay rising gracefully above the horizon.

An illusion, Sheeb thought. In fact, the mythological significance ascribed to the constellations was nothing more than a fabrication created in the minds of men. The stars that made up Ursa Major were thousands of light years apart. Their physical connection with each other in the night sky was only seen, as viewed from Earth. From other vantage points in the universe, the connections were not seen. And though their locations in the stellar sea were used by ancients mariners, their mythological significance was imposed. There was, in truth, no more significance between the stars that drew their mythological outlines in the sky than the furthest stars in yet unseen galaxies. In the chaos of the cosmos, man had found a way to navigate the seas and predict the rhythms of nature. In his desperation to create meaning, early man had emblazoned within the dark sky the stuff of his myths and dreams. Mankind had projected his deepest fears and aspirations onto an impersonal universe, Sheeb assured himself.

Had Sheeb drawn a picture of Ran in that same way? Had he seen only what he wished to see? No, it could not be. The man he remembered was real. Whatever had happened to Ran, whatever he had become, did not negate that truth. And yet what had happened? Reading the dossier enroute to the shuttle port, Sheeb had searched the archeology of word and symbol for a past he had not shared. The broken fragments of experience could only be hinted at.

After leaving Stanford, Ran had wound up in the New Mexico desert at Ecstasis. Carved from the inner mesas of the desert, Ecstasis was rumored to have had over ten thousand pilgrims, as they called themselves, each one professing to believe in a world of Light and striving to free themselves from this world of darkness.

The roots of the Ecstatics went back to the virtual beginnings of Christendom, except that then they were called Gnostics. The Gnostics believed in direct revelation of God without the need for priests or priestesses, and the Ecstatics carried forward this arcane heretical vision.

The Ecstatics had added a modern sacrament to their cosmological hodgepodge—the taking of psylocibin mushrooms. Taken in high doses, the natural hallucinogen transported the Ecstatics to unearthly vistas. The highest point of mushroom intoxication was called Strophoria, and it was during Strophoria that pilgrims were most likely to make contact with the Lords of Light themselves. Usually such contact was experienced only if a pilgrim had gone through a period of fasting and purification; then on the day of "communion," one's first and only meal would consist of the actual mushrooms and several hours of listening to Gregorian chants.

A pilgrim would then "soar," as they called it, upward to the heavenly realms on the wings of the bombastically loud medieval music. Upon contact with the Lords of Light, pilgrims would enter a state of utter stillness and would sit in direct communion with what they believed to be the most evolved beings in the universe. The cult had been disbanded by the government years ago. Forget freedom of religion. Too many young and brilliant minds had disappeared into the New Mexico desert.

Two years after Ran had entered as a novitiate, a federal raid of the monastery ended his quest for the Lords of Light. The next year or so was sketchy. For a brief period he worked as a lab technician at Indiana University, tending mice for medical experiments. His doctorate in neuropsychology had seemingly gone to waste.

The next clear report showed him in New York City. He had taken up residence with two women, reputedly priestesses for the local Rashtans. For the next year or two, he "serviced" them and worked part-time as a sales clerk in a Lower Manhattan occult bookstore. It was also during this period that he joined a secret group that purportedly worked with a system of strenuous mental exercises developed by the nineteenth-century mystic and magician Gurdjieff. The effects of this training on Ran were unknown.

Just before he was to be initiated and scarred by the Rashtans, he disappeared. Six months later he was living as a hermit in the now vacant monastery of Ecstasis in New Mexico. For the next three years, Ran lived alone. There were no records about what happened during this time, only vague reports from reservation Indians. Locals rumored that he had been seen roaming the hills with wild coyotes, and some said that they had stumbled upon him in deserted canyons levitating small boulders, apparently for fun. Whatever happened, Ran had shown up in San Francisco, alone and broke. He had applied for a position in a parapsychological experiment and had tested higher on the HewMatthews scale than anyone ever previously recorded. He was hired on the spot.

After six months of training and indoctrination, he had been placed as head of the research team by Hellenstat. The Mind War Machine had found its progenitor.

"So Ran must be a pretty interesting guy." Vollen's voice broke the silence. Sheeb glanced his way.

"Yeah, things were always pretty interesting with Ran." Sheeb turned back and looked out the portal. The shuttle was nearing Hawaii. Beneath them, Sheeb could see the placid waters of the Pacific through pink puffs of cumulus. His thoughts returned to Ran who had always wanted to live on the Kona coast, something about the warmth and turquoise water.

A leviathan of sadness overtook Sheeb once again. What would he say when he saw Ran? What would he feel when he touched him? A deep desolation took over him. Sensing his mood, Centauri nosed up against his thigh. Vollen's hand scratched the dog's ears, as did Sheeb's. Their hands met, and slight smiles broke across both their faces.

The computer signaled the ten-second alert. The shuttle would be decelerating for re-entry shortly. Vollen turned to his controls, though the procedure was fully automated.

Sheeb and Vollen were thrown back in their seats as the shuttle unexpectedly accelerated. Something was wrong. The main engines, used only for lift-off, were being activated. The craft shook from the torque of its powerful motors. Vollen reached for the manual override, but the computer would not relinquish control. His fist hit the arm rest, "Shit!"

"What's happening?"

"We're fucked, that's what!"

"Can you be a little more specific?" Sheeb asked, perturbed.

"The launch motors are firing, and I can't override the damn computer."

Vollen radioed Central Aeronautics Control for help as he frantically tried to shut down the engines. The radio was dead. By the time CAC noticed them rocketing away from Earth, it would be too late.

Cursing, Vollen punched in a series of commands to the computer, beads of sweat dripping from his forehead. Moments later the engines shut off, and the craft, now silent, shot into the darkness.

Manually re-routing the flight deck to his command, Vollen nosed Alpha Lyra around with its side jets. The craft was now hurtling into space backward. Switching the power boosters on, the two men braced them-selves...nothing. Something had happened to the Rockwells. Vollen cursed.

Punching in on-board teleme-try, Vollen anxiously watched the computer screen. There had been a short in the Pulse Regulator. He would have to go out-side for repairs. After spitting last-minute directions for moni-toring the various systems, Vollen crawled into the air lock. Pulling his helmet over his head and fastening it securely, Vollen activated the port command on the side wall. The steel hatch closed, and Vollen looked upward to the round hatch that had started to open.

Through the opening, Vollen watched the backdrop of stars sweeping above him. Pushing himself upward, the zero gravity of space carried him through the cylindrical canal, out into the starry vastness.

Vollen attached his tether to the side of the craft and pulled himself along the aluminum skin of the craft to the rear of the shuttle. Beneath him, puffs of cloud, far below, were lit up with the light of dawn.

How easy it would be to just let go... just let go of the tether and leave the strange Earth below him far behind. How easy it would be to drift away from the place where he had never felt at home.

Vollen chuckled at himself. He had had these same fantasies before, and he knew himself well enough to know he would never act on them, at least not as long as he was on a mission.

Finally reaching the control panel, Vollen pulled himself around and braced himself against one of the struts. He slid the cover back and peered inside. There was the problem. When he had taken manual control of the shuttle from the computer, static electricity back-charged into the highly sensitive Pulse Regulator. But why? There wasn't a technical reason that made sense unless someone had tampered with the firing systems.

Tapping off the excess charge from the PR unit, Vollen pulled the cover closed and headed back for the entry hatch. As he prepared to arch himself into the round opening, he took one last look. The stars enveloped him, their relentless silence echoing in his skull.

Pulling himself over into the waiting hatch, Vollen gently dropped toward the bottom of the tube his mind drifting off into a fantasy. Alone, above the Earth, Vollen turned slowly in the dark night of space as tears rolled from his eyes for the man who had never felt at home on the planet far beneath him. But no matter, the greater excitement of escape was pulling him, an excitement he could not and would not contain. He ripped the mask from his face, and breathed in the sweet nothingness of space, the stellar vacuum filling his lungs and pulling every shred of oxygen from his chest. Eyes dilated from the shock of sudden death, and Vollen drifted deeper and deeper into the womb of the Dark Mother...deeper and deeper into the eternal womb of space.

Vollen brought himself back to reality just in time to avoid crashing into the lower hatch. Pulling himself upright, he punched in the command to close the shaft. Glancing upward at the starry night beyond the closing hatch, Vollen took a deep breath and chuckled.

CHAPTER SEVENTEEN

He er power boosters repaired, Alex Vollen eased Alpha Lyra through the first ephemeral layers of the atmosphere. Vollen was double-checking all the controls when he broke the silence. "Damn close up there, Sheeb."

"I'm just glad it was you out there on the tether and not me," Sheeb offered.

"You don't like space walking?" Vollen asked incredulously.

"Never have done it," Sheeb responded.

"You don't know what you're missing."

"Maybe so, but I prefer solid ground."

Looking down to Earth through the port window, Sheeb could make out the coast of California. As the shuttle descended to 2,000 feet, he could see the distinctive plume of whales as they migrated south for the waters off Mexico. A blur of dark caught his eye; a flock of Canadian geese was on the wing, their regal necks outstretched into the air. The lead goose suddenly flew onto its side, veering west and then south again. Each bird followed behind as if the entire flock had been thrown into a spontaneous ballet, each movement of wing perfectly choreographed.

Sheeb looked back at the hump-backs. Deep within the cell minds of the mammoth cetaceans beneath him, a mysterious power was pulling them to their yearly rituals in Mexican waters, the same power that propelled the feathered geese toward South America.

Vollen threw a series of switches and the shuttle's landing gear slipped out from beneath its belly as the craft dropped to 500 feet. As the craft neared the ground, Vollen pulled back on the flaps and the stubby wings lost their lift. A young man from the lab was waiting for them as they pulled up to the hangar. The embroidered name tag on his silver jumpsuit read "Jeff/Motor Pool."

As Vollen and Sheeb stepped out of the shuttle, the lanky young man held out his hand. "Welcome back, Mr. Vollen."

They shook hands, and Vollen introduced him to Sheeb. Jeff nodded perfunctorily and walked to the rear of the Land Transport. The back of the Land Transport opened, and a droid rolled out onto the asphalt parking area. Jeff pointed to the shuttle. "Unload it." The droid answered in a highly mechanical voice, "Unloading now."

As the droid rolled its way over to the cargo doors, Centauri sauntered beside it, sniffing its metallic exterior. Lifting one of the larger bags, the droid kept bumping it into one of the doors of the LT. Jeff careened around the corner of the Transport, yelling at the droid. "You fucking piece of shit! Can't you do anything right?" He wrestled the bag from the droid and shoved it into the back of the Transport. "Fucking battery-operated intelligence. They should send you back to the junkyard!"

The droid responded in its typical mechanized nasal drone. "Junkyard? Please define junkyard."

"Oh, just shut up." Jeff motioned the droid into the cargo area. "Enter cargo area and secure yourself."

The droid rolled up into the LT. "Entering cargo area." Jeff shot the squat machine the bird and then slammed the door shut.

"So, are we ready?" Jeff looked at Vollen and Sheeb. Vollen nodded.

As they stepped inside and took their seats, the droid acknowledged the last part of Jeff's command. "Secure."

Jeff didn't say a word. Sheeb looked back and saw that the droid had rolled itself into a containment device. Centauri had jumped onto the back seat next to Sheeb. Sheeb let an arm rest on the dog's back as they pulled out of the shuttle port.

As the LT entered the freeway, Jeff pushed a laser disc into the stereo. The air suddenly pulsed with the heavy sounds of the Vulvonics, an all-woman neo-punk band from Germany that had just risen to the pinnacle of international acclaim. Their new single, "Wet Down to My Toes," reverberated through the LT as it headed for the coastal highway. No conversation was possible, only the driven heat of the Vulvonics. Finally the album ended, and Jeff pulled the laser disc from the stereo.

Vollen turned in his seat to face Jeff. "So, how have things been since I left?"

The aloof young man shrugged his shoulders. "I don't really know, you know. I just keep the motor pool running. As for the rest of the place, I could care less."

Vollen turned back around and they rode the rest of the way in silence. The road became narrower, and large trees hung their pendulous branches high above the pavement.

"There it is." Jeff pointed to an ornate stone wall and entrance. As they pulled the LT up to the guard station, the security officer stepped up to the driver's side and peered in.

"Okay." He motioned them through.

The driveway curled back on itself, winding its way down into a small valley like some giant snake. Mammoth ferns, some as high as thirty feet, clustered close to the drive. The air suddenly turned green and moist. Centauri sat up and poked his head out the window. He sniffed the air as if drinking some kind of nectar. Sheeb's mind was suddenly filled with the subtle nuances of aromas that he hadn't noticed at first.

Vollen leaned over from the front seat. "You know, Sheeb, botanists still can't figure out how this guy Bosk was able to create this." Vollen's hand floated through the air as if encircling the strange primeval forest.

The LT banked hard as Jeff pulled into a switchback. The air turned darker as the foliage grew thicker and large vines twisted themselves down from the roofs of trees. For a moment Sheeb imagined a giant prehistoric lizard slithering its way through the undergrowth. He was startled out of his reverie by a large expanse of green and pink. The LT had come across a monstrous planting of orchids. Looking closer, Sheeb could see that they weren't orchids at all, but thousands upon thousands of Venus Fly Traps. The carnivorous plants quivered in the slight breeze, their opened mouths waiting.

Vollen turned back from the front seat again. "Some people say that Bosk created a four-foot version of those things. Can you imagine? A plant able to swallow a small dog or a baby."

"That's pretty terrifying," Sheeb said.

"Yeah," Jeff added, slapping the dashboard with a free hand, "but only if you're a small dog or a baby." Vollen glanced at Jeff with an expression of disbelief, and then turned back in his seat.

"We're almost there." Jeff pointed toward an opening in the dense foliage.

Framed by a large canopy of dark ferns, the road veered into the open space of the estate grounds. A few hundred feet away, the concrete amoeba-like Bosk mansion sprawled across several acres. Driving up to the main entrance, one felt engulfed by the monstrous flying wings of glass and stone arching down to the earth from the roof of the solarium on the third floor. Perfectly trimmed roses clustered about the circular driveway, and the massive wooden door to the entrance reminded Sheeb of a medieval castle.

"Glastonbury," Vollen offered.

"What?" Sheeb asked.

"I saw you admiring the door. It's from a castle in Glastonbury from the fifteenth century. Bosk was quite the collector."

Getting out of the LT, Sheeb glanced upward to the shimmer of light from the solarium. A voice startled him from behind.

"You must be Alan Sheeb. I'm Ellen Darkos." The woman extended her hand. Black hair with the faintest whisperings of gray had been pulled back behind her head in a tight bun. Everything about her, from her Lauren suit to the sterling silver brooch pinned so as to follow the line of her collar, spelled control.

"So, did you have a pleasant trip?"

"Yes," he replied.

"Good." Darkos glanced at Vollen with a perfunctory nod. "Alex."

Turning to Sheeb, Darkos motioned towards the large entrance. "Now, if you'll follow me to my office, I'll fill you in on some things before you get settled."

"Certainly." Sheeb walked toward the main entrance, Centauri and Vollen following behind.

"And what is that?" Darkos pointed to the dog.

"Oh, that's Centauri," Sheeb said.

"I don't allow dogs in my office."

Sheeb motioned Centauri onto the grounds. "Go play. I'll come for you later."

Darkos led Sheeb and Vollen into the main building of the Bosk compound. The director's office was off from the large oval room which they had just entered. Stepping into her office, Darkos motioned both of them to sit down.

Sheeb took a seat in front of her mahogany desk, next to Vollen. Darkos lowered herself into her leather chair and reached for a folder on her desk. Sheeb noticed something moving from the corner of his eye. Turning, he saw a large Galapagos lizard slithering its way to the glass walls of a giant terrarium.

"Interesting creature over there." Sheeb nodded towards the lizard.

"Yes." Darkos looked at him quizzically.

"Mind if I look?"

"Not at all." Darkos rose from her chair and crossed the room towards the reptile.

"It's magnificent," Sheeb said.

"Yes, in their own way," Darkos cocked her head to one side, "they are quite admirable. I appreciate their efficiency and lack of emotions."

Darkos caught the glimmer of surprise in Sheeb's eyes. She turned back to her desk, indicating that the zoological side trip had come to an end. Motioning Sheeb and Vollen back to their seats, Darkos opened the folder in front of her. She looked at Sheeb.

"I assume that Vollen has thoroughly briefed you on Dr. Farr's condition."

Sheeb nodded.

"How long do you think it will take to get a preliminary assessment?"

"That depends."

"Depends on what?" Darkos asked.

"It depends on how quickly I can get rapport with him."

Darkos put a hand to her chiseled jaw. "I suggest you do it quickly. We haven't much time. There's a lot of pressure from above to get this thing resolved." Darkos leafed through the folder and pulled out several sheets. She passed the papers across the desk to Sheeb. "I'm in charge here." Darkos cocked her head to the side, the same way she had done earlier by the caged reptile. "Surely you can appreciate the situation that puts me in."

Sheeb's words were highly calculated. "I understand. I'll get control of the situation as soon as possible." With the word control, Sheeb cocked his head ever so slightly to the same side and in the same way Darkos had done earlier. Darkos's right eye slightly dilated. For a moment, time seemed suspended. Darkos cleared her throat, suddenly aware that something had slipped past her.

"The papers you are holding in your hands are the last observation reports on Dr. Farr. I have had him monitored twenty-four hours a day on closed-circuit television. I hope the reports will prove helpful."

"I'm sure they will," Sheeb said.

"Any questions?"

Sheeb shook his head.

"Good. I'd like to talk with Vollen for a few moments, and then I'll have him escort you up to the solarium. That's where Dr. Farr spends most of his time."

Sheeb stood up and headed for the door.

"Oh, and Dr. Sheeb..."

"Yes?" Sheeb turned to face Darkos.

"Get back to me as soon as you know anything."

"Absolutely."

Darkos motioned him to the door.

Stepping out into the oval room, Sheeb walked past the receptionist's desk and took a seat on one of the large overstuffed couches. An original painting of water lilies by Monet hung on the far wall, the mysteriously ill-defined edges of the flowers floating in a sea of mist. The reports of the last three days were just as mysterious and ill-defined. All of the information had been gleaned from closed-circuit television observations. Ran was continuing in his silence. Sheeb spent the next several minutes looking over the reports in detail, but there was nothing.

Looking up from the papers, Sheeb noticed a large ceramic dragon sitting on a mahogany table next to the wall. The detail was superb, with the lustrous finish indicative of the high Ming period. Sheeb's thoughts went back to the lizard in Darkos's office. The animal had been genetically altered, its green eyes betraying the secret. For a few moments, Sheeb thought of Darwin on his expedition to the islands of Galapagos, drifting off the waters of Equador.

The door opened to the director's office. Darkos and Vollen stepped out into the reception area. "A phone call for you, Ms. Darkos." The receptionist held the phone aloft.

"Who is it?" Darkos asked.

"Jeff. He wants to know if you need him for anything."

Darkos crossed to the desk. "Jeff, I want those motor pool reports redone."

Sheeb had only a moment, only a second, to drop in sync and find out what Darkos was hiding. Diving into her nervous system was like dropping through molecules of titanium steel. Nothing gave way. Scanning an energy tunnel that led down into the limbic core, Sheeb felt a tidal wave of rage. It pulsed upward toward the conscious areas of the brain, only to be pushed back again into the core by a barrage of catecholamines.

Sensing Sheeb scanning her, Darkos turned and glanced his way. He quickly backed off from the limbic tunnel and pulled his awareness from her brain.

Darkos placed the receiver back in its cradle, and turned to Vollen. "Take Dr. Sheeb up to the solarium to meet Dr. Farr."

Sheeb pulled himself from the couch, and followed Vollen to the glass elevator. As they rode to the arched roof of the solarium in silence, Sheeb noticed Darkos eyeing him.

CHAPTER EIGHTEEN

Darkos continued to stare at Sheeb until he disappeared into the platinum and glass tube that carried him and Vollen to the Solarium. She pulled a folder from the top of the Plexiglas reception desk, the folder seeming oddly heavier than she remembered.

Pulling her body into her office, Darkos felt like she was dragging herself up the side of a mountain. The Director closed the door behind her. At her desk, Darkos opened a drawer and pulled the telecomputer to her face. She anxiously punched in the access codes, and waited for the microwaves to find their way to the North American Telecom Satellite. The faint glitches marked their connection with the massive communications station. Most calls originating in the Americas were routed through such orbiting links.

Darkos reached over and punched in the scrambler. Should her call be intercepted, the conversation would be reduced to a mess of static, blips, voice inversions, and frequency interference. The last of the glitches sounded in the background of line static. The waves had been routed to Washington.

"Hello." Charles Buchner's voice sounded rushed.

"What happened?"

"Ellen?"

"Yes."

"What do you mean, what happened?"

"Both Vollen and Sheeb were just in my office."

"That's impossible. Their dead bodies are on their way to Mars by now."

"Well, something went wrong. They're here."

Buchner sighed. "All right, Ellen. I suppose I'll have to attend to this personally. I'll be there within forty-eight hours."

"Two days?" Darkos's voice betrayed her frustration.

"I'm in the midst of very critical negotiations for the government, and it's impossible for me to leave until they are completed."

Irked by the turn of events, Darkos's eyes darted about the room.

"Can you manage to keep Sheeb in the dark until I get there?" Buchner asked.

"I guess I'll have to," Darkos said weakly.

"Kill him if you have to, Ellen. I'm counting on you."

Darkos's mind floated for a moment, avoiding his words. For an instant she fantasized about the telecom satellite and tried to imagine how it was linking her and Charles Buchner, as if by thinking about something so far away she might avoid the immediacy of her situation.

Unknown to her, in the microchip handling her call to Buchner, two streams of electrons were flowing side by side, no more than a micron apart. Two conversations from different locations were being processed together. Darkos's words with Buchner had been broken down into digital sequences, each group of electrons representing a vowel, a consonant, a plosive. Tucked beside it, another conversation ensued. A young boy calling from his parents' apartment in New York was talking excitedly with his grandfather half a world away in Australia. The two electronic rivers flowed side by side, so close yet so different. Through one flowed the syntax of life, in the other a river of death.

"Ellen, did you hear me?" Buchner asked. "I said kill him if he gets in the way."

"Yes, I heard you." Darkos's voice betrayed her frustration.

Without missing a beat, Buchner's voice suddenly took on a conciliatory tone, a tone Darkos recognized as a calculated attempt to assuage her doubts about the unexpected turn of events. "I already have a buyer for the device, Ellen; all of us are going to be very rich."

Images of a villa by the Italian Riviera drifted through Darkos. Leaning back in her chair for a moment, she could almost feel the caress of the Mediterranean. Bringing herself back to the room, Darkos stood up and reached to her head, smoothing a stray hair back into place.

"I'm counting on you, Ellen."

"Yes, Charles, I know."

The line went dead, and Darkos slipped the receiver back into its small black case. She stood for the longest time just staring at the floor, her hands to her face. A thump in the corner of the room pulled her attention from the carpet. The giant lizard had found the tiny

frog she had placed in the terrarium earlier. The small amphibian had been cornered by the massive reptile and was frantically
trying to escape.

The terrified animal kept bump-
ing into the sides of the glass prison. Darkos walked over to the
struggle and sat on one of the stools beside the large habitat.
The Galapagos moved itself within a few inches of the tiny creature, the lizard's pink tongue whipping the air.

Darkos watched the spectacle,
unable to enter fully into the enjoyment she usually experienced
at feeding time. There was too much on her mind. The turn of
events had placed her in jeopardy, and the only one she could
count on was herself.

It was then she realized how
angry she was with Buchner. What did he mean, kill Sheeb?
Didn't he realize the administrative nightmare it would bring
down on her?

Darkos felt her rage rise like
steam from heated rocks as the Galapagos closed in for the kill.
The massive lizard's raspy tongue slid up and around the tiny
leg of the terrified creature, pulling the amphibian's frantic body
toward it.

Easy enough for Buchner to
say what to do, safely tucked away within the U.S. government. Darkos slid her hands down her thighs as she gazed
into the terrified eyes of the small frog. Darkos felt trapped,
and it was a feeling she didn't like. She had to do something,
but what?

The lizard's sharp teeth ripped
into the amphibian's soft body, and a stream of urine mixed
with blood dripped down the frog's quivering leg. The reptile
threw its head back into the air and swallowed the dying creature head first. Only its padded toes remained in the air, shaking

uncontrollably. There was the sound of a soft crunch as the lizard crushed the frog's skull. The toes ceased their movement and the lizard swallowed the rest of the creature into its acid-filled belly. The Galapagos moved its head to one side and stared at its captor through the thick glass of the terrarium, as if it yearned to devour her as well. Taking a breath, Darkos stood and walked back toward her desk.

Sliding into her leather arm-chair, Darkos pulled the report from its folder. Since yesterday, she had asked for six-hour updates on Ran. The most recent surveillance took up a mere two pages of white paper, now held between her fingers.

Farr...Of course. The solution to her dilemma was not knocking off Sheeb as Buchner had suggested, but lay instead in the brain chemistry of Dr. Farr himself. In her excitement, Darkos picked up a mechanical pencil and gently tapped the ledger pad on her desk. Recalling a conversation she had had with the director of Biological Resources, she remembered his comment about neurotransmitters and memory. The former MIT professor had developed a neuro-transmitter block for the CIA that erased memory.

The recipient of such a block would forget everything until an antidote was administered. The drug had been created under a grant and was now being given to field agents on a regular basis for the unlikely event of their capture. Not even the Deep Mind Probes could capture the suppressed memory patterns locked within its biochemical net.

Darkos reached over to her interoffice phone. Tapping in the sequence of numbers, she watched the giant Galapagos in the corner of the room as it lay against the glass sides of its prison. Its membranous eyes were closed, the digestion of the frog in its belly drawing blood from its brain and pulling it into a deep slumber.

"Biological Resources."

"Dr. Hoffman, please."

"And who may I say is calling?"

"Ellen Darkos."

"Oh, Ms. Darkos, Dr. Hoffman isn't here at the moment." The woman's voice seemed suddenly frantic. "He's in the solarium giving Dr. Farr his vitamin injections. Shall I have him call you as soon as he returns?" she asked.

"Yes, please do." Darkos hung up the phone.

It was more than twenty minutes before Hoffman returned her call.

"Ms. Darkos, how may I help you?" he asked.

Darkos did not like to wait, and her voice did not conceal her frustration. "I would like to see you in my office as soon as possible."

There was a pause at the other end. "Okay. Anything I should know beforehand?"

"Yes, as a matter of fact. Bring your notes on Memorol 57."

"You do realize it's a classified drug?"

"Yes, Dr. Hoffman, I do."

"But I don't have any notes on Memorol 57."

"Surely you have mental notes. After all, you did invent it."

"Well, yes, but..."

"I assure you that our conversation won't go any further than the two of us."

"You're the director."

"Thank you. In a few minutes then?" Darkos asked in her most pleasant voice.

"That's fine."

"Good. I'll be waiting for you."

Hoffman hung up and the line went dead.

Darkos smiled inwardly at herself. Ran Farr's mind would soon be in her possession, and there was nothing Sheeb, not even talented Sheeb, could do to stop her.

CHAPTER NINETEEN

Vollen and Sheeb rode the elevator in silence, Sheeb pressing himself against the side as they rode upward to the solarium. Vollen broke the silence.

"Curious woman."

"There is something very odd about her, isn't there?"

Vollen nodded, his hand gently stroking the steel handrail. "An unsatisfied woman is a dangerous thing, Sheeb." They both laughed, and for a moment their eyes met. The twinkle in their eyes at the humor of Vollen's observation was one of those confidences between men, those moments of tacit agreement about an event or situation where the gulf between strangers is bridged by a common observation. "How long have you known her?" Sheeb asked.

"About six months. She was the project director when Bach brought me on board."

"So," Sheeb asked. "who is actually in charge?"

"She's in charge of the project, but I'm the director of security and I have direct authority from Bach. In that regard I have the ultimate authority."

"She knows this?" Sheeb asked.

"Yes, and she doesn't like it." Vollen offered. "She likes to be in contro—total control."

"I noticed," Sheeb added. "But it seems there's more to this than just her need for control. It's like she can hardly tolerate you."

Vollen laughed. "Very astute Sheeb. Our stand-off goes back to my first few days here. She tried to throw her weight around, and I called her on it. When she wouldn't back off, I called Bach. Within hours, the president of Hellenstat was here himself. He raked Darkos over the coals, humiliating her in front of the entire staff." Vollen nodded as the elevator came to rest at the third-floor solarium. "We're here." The glass doors slid back, and waving his hand, he motioned Sheeb through.

Vollen led him down a light-filled corridor to the massive rooftop botanical garden. The glassed-in roof looked out over Weirman Lake, an extraordinary body of water that Bosk had built to resemble the fjords of Norway. Looking at the intriguing landscape gave the impression of being in another world altogether.

At the end of the long hallway, sensors picked up their approach and a blue-tinted glass door slid open. The two of them stepped through, and Vollen led Sheeb to a large planting of ferns in the middle of a clearing.

Ran was sitting turned away from them. A flannel shirt lay crumpled at his feet. The pink of Ran's skin seemed oddly transparent. It wasn't that Sheeb could see through him, but rather an impression that he could.

The door to the solarium slid open and Sheeb turned to see who had entered. Vollen held out his hand. "Dr. Hoffman, I'd like you to meet Dr. Sheeb. He's the deprogrammer we brought in to work with Dr. Farr."

The nondescript man in the white lab coat held out his hand and glanced at Sheeb momentarily. "Nice to meet you, doctor—and now, if you gentlemen will excuse me..." Hoffman motioned toward Ran still staring at an orchid, and seemingly oblivious of the conversation.

"Of course." Vollen stepped back a bit to let Hoffman through, and then turned to Sheeb. "He gives Dr. Farr vitamin and nutrient shots several times a day. Ran hasn't eaten in weeks, and the shots keep his vitality up."

"Very good," Sheeb said.

For the next several minutes, Sheeb and Vollen watched as Hoffman pulled a syringe from his black medical bag and injected Ran with a colorless liquid.

"Exactly what is the composition of the injection?" Sheeb asked.

Hoffman looked up as he returned the syringe to its holder. "A combination of simple sugars, vitamins, minerals, and electrolytes. I have found that whatever state Dr. Farr is in, it burns up B-complex, vitamin C, and electrolytes at an unbelievable rate. To be on the safe side, I also take blood tests every day to make sure that we are supplying Dr. Farr with what he needs."

"Thank you, Dr. Hoffman." Vollen interjected, noting that he and Sheeb wished to be alone with Ran.

Hoffman nodded and closed his bag. He left the solarium without so much as a word or a second glance.

"He pretty much keeps to himself," Vollen offered.

Turning his attention back to Ran, Sheeb had that strange feeling again, as if Ran were somehow translucent. Shaking himself from the impression, Sheeb touched Vollen on the shoulder. "Would you mind leaving us alone?"

"No, not at all. When you're done, just come to my office down the hall. It's the seventh door on the left." Vollen pointed to the doors at the other end of the solarium.

Sheeb nodded, and Vollen turned and walked behind the ferns that surrounded them. Sheeb heard the glass door to the solarium open and close as Vollen left.

Out in the corridor, Vollen raised a hand to his shoulder where Sheeb had touched him. To be touched was not something Vollen often experienced. He put up a wall of aloofness about himself wherever he went, and few were able to pierce it. But something about this Sheeb guy had managed to reach him. Chastising himself for his weakness, Vollen walked down the hall toward his quarters. Something about the incident with Sheeb struck him as familiar irony, but what? Vollen searched his mind, as he might search a client's files. He left no thought unturned, but he did not find "it," for he was looking in the wrong place. The clue was not in his mind but in his body, a body that simply and exquisitely longed to be touched. Nothing more, nothing less. This simple truth had eluded Vollen for his entire life.

When he reached the door to his quarters, Vollen punched in the entry code and the steel door slid open. Walking across the slate-gray carpet to the electronic monitoring equipment, he noticed that the computer was flashing a communications alert. Within the last fifteen minutes, Darkos had sent a scrambled message to Washington.

"Interesting." Vollen spoke out loud to the array of electronics as if they might understand him.

146

Sitting down in front of the console, Vollen punched in the computer access code. As the computer relinquished its vast domain to his fingers, Vollen felt the pleasure of having outwitted Darkos. He had instinctively mistrusted Darkos upon first meeting her. He had snuck into her office several months earlier, and found the scrambler in a drawer. He had deciphered the code and then returned the device to its dark cradle, waiting for the day when Darkos would use it.

Sitting back in his chair, Vollen peered at the screen before him as the computer decoded the oscillating waves of information mixed with interference. As he waited for the deciphered message to be printed, his mind wandered back to Sheeb. What was he doing now, alone, with Ran amidst the ferns?

Vollen switched on the closed-circuit television and turned on the monitor to the solarium. A silent picture came into view. Neither Ran nor Sheeb were speaking. Sheeb had just moved closer, sitting down in front of Ran. Ran seemed not to notice him. Vollen adjusted the camera slightly to get a better view.

Looking up, Sheeb noticed one of the cameras on the far wall rotating toward him on its axis. He suppressed an urge to walk over and smash it to pieces. Instead, he crossed his legs in front of Ran, who continued gazing into an inordinately large opalescent orchid. Sheeb looked into his friend's transfixed eyes. The pupils were dilated, and Ran seemed totally unaware of Sheeb's presence.

Sheeb felt a strange energy coming off of Ran. It reminded him of that mysterious feeling he had experienced while swimming with the dolphins back on Christos. The odd feelings were drawing Sheeb into a kind of reverie, the ferns and orchids around them suddenly seeming more beautiful. The odd energy coming from Ran was calling Sheeb into a strange and enchanting new world. But it was a world Sheeb could not afford to enter. He needed his objectivity, and so he began to mentally assess Ran's condition. Pulling a light pencil from his pocket, Sheeb moved closer and directed the thin beam of light into Ran's right retina. Nothing; the eyes were not responding to light. Ran's brain had not, it seemed, even registered the stimulation. Whatever had happened to Ran, it must have been of a titanic nature to create such catatonia.

Slipping the light pencil back into his pocket, Sheeb decided to take advantage of Ran's condition. Without any of the usual inhibitors operating in Ran's consciousness, it would be easy to drop in sync and track him. In a sense, it was easier for Sheeb to deal with Ran in this condition. Sheeb could be more detached. The man in front of him was not the friend who disappeared ten years ago. Something radical had happened, and not just the psychotic break. It was something else. Sheeb could see it in his face.

Shifting into deep alpha, Sheeb dropped into sync and dove into the waters of Ran's mind. Ran's brain was pumping endorphins into the bloodstream, his pleasure centers buzzing and hissing with the heightened chemical liqueur of natural opiates. The endorphin levels had risen so high that the deeper strata of the brain were reeling from intoxication. That would certainly explain his nonresponse to the light pencil, but where were his memory patterns? Where was the secret of the Mind War Machine being stored?

Ran seemed totally immobilized by the shock of whatever had happened to him. The psychotic break had gone very deep into the underlying physical structures of the psyche itself. It could only be guessed at, but it looked to Sheeb as if Ran's system was trying to compensate by flooding its own pleasure centers with waves of endorphins, creating a kind of neurological Mardi Gras to mask over some deeply hidden pain and shock. If Sheeb was correct, he would find the secret to what happened sealed away in the deeper structures of the brain itself.

Sheeb was adjusting his angle of descent into the hippocampus, a major site for memory, when he heard Ran talking to him. Sheeb opened his eyes and looked over at Ran. He hadn't moved, and he was still staring at the monstrously huge orchid. Nothing in particular had changed, Sheeb noted, and so he turned his attention inward, once again.

"So you finally came."

Ran's words, Sheeb realized, were being spoken from within his own mind. Not knowing quite how to handle the odd experience, Sheeb thought back his response to Ran. "How did you know I was coming?"

"I felt it. Sheeb, have you ever noticed how beautiful an orchid truly is? There's an entire universe in every molecule. It's incredible Sheeb. It really is."

Sheeb decided to amuse Ran by looking at the large flower in front of them. Opening his eyes, he surveyed the rare Amazonian botanical. Its nearly white edges turned ruby red as they folded into the flower's open throat. Golden-tipped stamen quivered in the air. He hadn't remembered seeing the orchid this beautiful when he had first sat down. But now it scintillated, its colors pulsing into the room. Sheeb felt himself slipping somehow, as if the exotic flower were seducing him and drawing him into itself.

Ran spoke again, from somewhere, it seemed, inside Sheeb's brain. "It's breathtaking, isn't it? I can't find the end to it."

Sheeb gazed around the solarium. Everywhere he looked he felt himself being pulled into Ran's strange new world. What had first looked like ferns now seemed like vortexes of swirling green light reaching out as if wanting to touch him. Sheeb felt the flood of endorphins swirling through his own brain. Ran was activating something within him. Soon they'd both be stoned out of their minds. It felt like climbing up a sheer rock wall from a garden of unbelievable delight. Leaving behind him the ecstatic grandeur of Ran's new world, Sheeb forced himself out of deep alpha. He couldn't afford to lose himself in Ran's insanity.

As Sheeb returned to normal consciousness, he heard Ran calling to him, as if from some great distance.

"Will you come back?" he asked.

"Yes, Ran... I'll be back."

"I've missed you."

The warm words had cut a path into Sheeb's heart. Putting a hand to Ran's shoulder, he was overcome with feelings he had long ago shut away. Sheeb rose from the floor, and walked half-staggering to the glass door at the other end of the room.

Vollen glanced away from the monitor and turned his attention to the terminal in front of him. It was getting boring anyway. Sheeb and Ran hadn't said a word. As far as Vollen could tell, nothing had happened.

More interesting things were happening with the computer. It had decoded the scrambled message from Darkos to a Charles Buchner. Vollen punched in the command to print out the communication, the printer silently humming as it translated the language of electrons into printed words. Vollen pulled the finished transcript from the mouth of the feeder and leaned back in his chair. His suspicions had been correct. The accident on board Alpha Lyra had been planned.

But who is Charles Buchner and what is his relationship to the U.S. government? Vollen spun around in his chair and spoke into the computer's microphone, his words instantly translated into the electronic syntax of the language recognition program. "Acquire all information concerning Charles Buchner at the U.S. State Department. Priority Search." Vollen then punched in the security code that would shield his search from prying eyes.

Vollen rose from his chair and kicked the air. There was nothing that could be done until the information on Charles Buchner was retrieved. He could almost feel Darkos's neck breaking in his hands.

"Not now, not now." Vollen was pacing the room, talking out loud to the supple muscles of his body that yearned to kill the woman who would have had him exterminated. No, he must be cunning. He must not let his anger blind him. Better to wait and see the best path for revenge.

Vollen's rational mind certainly understood the need for discipline. Everything Vollen had ever achieved had been through the harsh sadhana of denial. But aching within every fiber of his body, an ancient warrior cried out to kill. It wanted the taste of Darkos's blood in its mouth. Vollen knew that it had to be fed or it would destroy his waiting.

Vollen stripped off his shirt and threw it into the corner of the room. He took a two-inch slab of wood that served as a shelf from its resting place, and he laid it across two file cabinets. Lowering himself to his knees, he clasped his hands and placed them on the solid board suspended between the two cabinets. In his imagination the board had become Darkos. Channeling the anger in his body, he raised his shaking arms in the air. Quivering with rage, Vollen's arms paused for a moment.

Vollen screamed, the air suddenly filled with blood. His arms crashed into the board, and in his mind Darkos fell to the floor, her back broken in two. Vollen dropped to the carpet. His hands stung with pain. His mouth filled with saliva, and in his imagination, it had changed to Darkos's blood.

CHAPTER TWENTY

The late afternoon sun had wandered its way westward. The sky, now a pastel of blue, would soon be on fire with the setting sun. Sheeb had walked downstairs from the Solarium, onto the enormous semi-circular stone patio that overlooked Weirman Lake, after his encounter with Ran. The vast lake stretched out before him, and off in the distance perhaps a mile or so, he could see the placid expanse of the Pacific Ocean. The air tasted of salt, and the heat of day was still radiating from the masonry under his feet.

To his right he could see the motor pool garage. Jeff was outside, shirtless, washing one of the LTs. A lone seagull hovered in the air, the white underbelly of its body luminescent in the late afternoon light of the sun. Sheeb folded his hands and leaned over the railing, staring off into the opaque water as if looking for something.

"What was that?" Sheeb thought to himself.

He had been so sure of Ran's psychosis, so sure of it. But that was before Ran had talked to him in his own mind. Now he didn't know. In fact, he didn't know a thing about Ran's condition. He had no maps for this territory of the psyche. And like an explorer grappling with some strange new land, he sensed an ominous danger. Ran's world was seductive and beautiful, so much so that it had taken every ounce of will for Sheeb to pull himself out of it.

Gazing off into the dark clouds just barely above the horizon, Sheeb wiped a tear from his eyes as he recalled Ran's last words: "I've missed you."

Hearing the soft padding of feet behind him, Sheeb turned to find Centauri sitting on his haunches. The animal sat poised and still, looking intently at his master.

"Jeez, I'm still in Ran's world," Sheeb thought. There was a soft but clearly recognizable light emanating from Centauri's chest. "Enough of this!" Reaching down and grabbing a stick from the deck, Sheeb called out to the dog. "Here, boy—fetch."

Sheeb tossed the stick in the air, but Centauri didn't move. Instead, he cocked his head to one side, and looked up at Sheeb. For the longest time Sheeb just stood there looking at the dog, and then something shifted; Sheeb was seeing himself through the eyes of the Valkovian. What he saw amazed and bedazzled him. It was as if he was standing in a cocoon of light. Different colors swirled about him, seemingly emanating from deep inside his own body. The spinning vortices within him looked like colored wheels turning with a power all their own. He recognized the odd phenomena as chakras. He had read about them as an undergraduate when he was studying Eastern methods of trance induction. But here he was seeing them for himself. Why hadn't he seen these before?

He was thinking about this strange paradox when he noticed something odd in his chest. It seemed that there was a blockage to the light radiating from his heart chakra, the vortex of light that sat behind the sternum. He recalled Kathrina saying that it was from here that people energetically felt emotion; it was from here that people felt love. And it was here that Sheeb was blocked. Ever the scientist, Sheeb decided to see if he could affect the strange light in his chest. He thought about Kathrina for a moment to see if anything would change. Nothing happened. But then he tried recalling the way he felt when he was with her. The warm feelings felt like flower petals opening in his chest, and to his amazement the "thing" blocking his heart began to retreat, and in its place a radiant ball of light began to appear.

Centauri stood on all fours and barked. The soft light Sheeb had seen earlier reappeared and streamed over from the dog's chest into Sheeb's now-open heart. Sheeb's eyes filled with tears, and the bushes around the patio began to shimmer with the same beauty that the orchids had shown in the solarium. Sheeb turned from Centauri and grabbed the railing. The world seemed to be spinning, and it was only through an act of sheer will that Sheeb was able to stop it. Finally he regained his composure and made a mental note to be more careful in his dealings with Ran's strange world. The success of the mission, he told himself, depended upon objectivity. To lose it would be the end of both Ran and himself.

As he gazed out across the water, the world slowly returned to normal. The shimmering energy had calmed, and Sheeb sighed with relief. Ran's new world was filled with terrors beyond imagining, terrors disguised as beauty and love. And no matter what it looked like, Ran was in a dangerous new world.

CHAPTER TWENTY-ONE

The reptile was in deep slumber, its white underbelly pressed against the glass wall of the terrarium. There was a slight rasping sound as the lizard exhaled through scaly nostrils. The slow and steady breathing of the creature had lulled Darkos into a light trance, her eyes transfixed by the rising and falling of the captive's chest. The lizard's right claw suddenly shredded and scraped the air, startling Darkos from her reverie. Leaning back against the wall, Darkos wondered if lizards dreamed.

A piece of lint on the floor caught her eye, and bending over to reach it, she noticed the reptile's hot breath against the glass wall. Unknown to Darkos, trapped within the water vapor of the lizard's exhale were thousands upon thousands of invisible electrons that had once been the eye of a frog. Those electrons were now spinning out across the room and into the air that Darkos breathed.

Darkos pressed a thumb to the glass opposite the small circle of fog. She leaned back, satisfied with herself. It somehow gave her immense pleasure to control such a large creature. Her thoughts returned to Hoffman. She had managed to cage him too. The thought pleased her.

Hoffman had once been one of the top biochemists in the country. He had gone to work at

MIT, where he and Stan Klaus had developed Memorol 57. The potent neurological suppressant had been the byproduct of their work in memory. When administered intravenously, Memorol wiped out the memory circuits of an individual so that the person would not even remember his name. The only antidote was Memorol 75A, an exact molecular replica of Memorol 57, only in reverse. When the two substances met inside the brain, they canceled each other out; the person regained his memory and the only known side effect was an excruciating headache.

Hoffman had had a promising career. There was talk of a Nobel Prize. Unfortunately, Hoffman had developed a taste for the euphoria of Endorphinol. He had synthesized it as a graduate student, sold it to fellow students, and became hooked himself. Endorphinol was classified as a MPE (Mega Pleasure Enhancer) Class 1. It was highly illegal and was one of the most controlled substances in the world. It could only be prescribed by a board of physicians for the terminally ill. Under the smallest doses of the drug, the dying passed into oblivion, stoned out of their minds, in utter bliss.

In the veins of healthy individuals, Endorphinol posed a major threat to society. Users would rather take the drug than work, eat, or sleep. As their bodies wasted away, their brains reeled under tidal waves of pleasure, making them ineffective and unproductive workers. It had recently become a capital crime to synthesize the drug, and offenders were summarily executed or imprisoned for life. When it was discovered that Hoffman was making the drug in the lab for his own use, he was asked to leave. Black-marked by the University Regents, he was barred from doing research ever again. To the Board it seemed an act of compassion to disbar Hoffman rather than turn him over to the authorities. To Hoffman, however, it was a ticket to purgatory.

His wife and children left him. Alone and almost destitute, he found himself at Hellenstat at the suggestion of a colleague. Just last week the Nobel Prize for Chemistry had been awarded in Zurich to Stan Klaus for his work with the Klaus Memory Matrix. Hoffman hadn't even been mentioned. It was as if he had never existed. His position with Hellenstat was the only one he would ever find, and he knew it.

For Darkos, the beauty of the situation was that Hoffman was indebted to her. Last year when the current position became vacant, a stream of candidates flowed through her office. She chose Hoffman not only for his impeccable scientific credentials and expertise, but also because his dark secret would allow her to manipulate him should the need ever arise.

Darkos had discovered quite some time ago that the art of manipulating others lay in giving them the illusion that their cages were larger than they really were. For Hoffman, this meant restoring a semblance of respect. He had lost so much of it. It must have been refreshing to the man to regain some dignity. Darkos had no problem with this, as long as it served her.

The intercom buzzed, and Darkos left the sleeping lizard for her desk. "Yes?"

"Dr. Hoffman is here to see you, ma'am."

"Send him in."

Darkos slipped behind the desk and into her leather armchair. The door opened, and a hesitant man in his late fifties entered the room.

"Doctor, please." Darkos motioned to one of the chairs in front of her.

The doctor sat in the chair, his hands in his lap, his right hand nervously fingering a button on his lab coat.

"I have a question, doctor."

"Yes?"

"Is it possible to synthesize Memorol 57 here in our lab?"

"I'm afraid," Hoffman cleared his throat, "that Memorol is a controlled substance. It is a felony to make it or any of its derivatives."

Darkos felt an impulse to say "as is Endorphinol," but decided against it. It might make Hoffman uncomfortably aware of his cage. She decided to take another route.

"As you realize, doctor, our lab is highly secret. No one other than you or I would know."

"What would it be used for...if I might ask?" Hoffman looked to the floor.

"I'm afraid I can't divulge that information just yet, but I assure you that it would only be in the interest of this project."

Hoffman stared at a slit of golden light on the floor that had wandered into the room through the slated blinds and onto the carpet.

"Yes...." his voice sounded far away.

"Yes, what?"

Hoffman knew there was no point in lying. If he lied and said no, she would ask for whatever it was he needed and have it delivered to the lab. Better to tell the truth and be done with it. "Yes, we have everything."

"That's wonderful, doctor." Darkos took a deep breath. Now came the art. Darkos looked at her fingernails as she spoke. "It would make my job a lot easier if you could help me with this. I pulled strings to get you here. I would think that the..."

"Ok, you'll have it. How soon do you need it?"

Darkos smiled. "As soon as possible."

"It takes twelve hours to distillate, three hours to centrifuge, and about another nine hours for the electromagnetic bonding... so I'd guess about twenty-four hours."

"I'd like you to start immediately. And I'd like it to be just our little secret."

"Well, you certainly have my agreement on that one, Ms. Darkos."

Hoffman rose from his chair and headed for the door. Opening it, he paused and looked at the sleeping lizard across the room. Darkos rose from behind her desk. "Oh, and doctor, thank you." She tried to make her voice sound as pleasant and as genuine as possible. Out in the hall, Hoffman mumbled to himself, "She probably fucks that thing at night."

CHAPTER TWENTY-TWO

Vollen lay sprawled on the floor, his right arm stretched out beneath him like a panther, his mind deep in sleep.

In his dream world, Vollen was somersaulting backwards. Moments before, Darkos had pulled a pulse laser from her purse and fired into his stomach, his flesh exploding into a flash of light and heat. Turning in his dream, Vollen saw that he was flying into the arms of the Dark Mother.

"I've been waiting for you." Her words echoed in the silent blackness of interstellar space. Her body, made from black holes and galaxies of dark stars, enfolded him, engulfing him in eternal night.

Drifting through millennia, Vollen watched as quasars died into fields of electromagnetic static. Galaxies birthed and died before him, the lives of whole worlds seemingly instantaneous, as if all of creation were but a heartbeat.

A piercing sound shattered the universe, and Vollen bolted upright. Groggy and still half in his dream world of dying stars, Vollen pulled himself from the floor and dragged his body to the computer. Information on the infamous Buchner was pouring onto the luminescent screen as the computer screeched its programmed alert into the room.

Vollen stared at the screen, rubbing his eyes. Charles Buchner was a high level attaché to the U.S. government. An investment capitalist, he held massive holdings in several international corporations. His position in government had given him tremendous covert abilities, and apparently he often used them. So why the Mind War Machine? Was he interested for intelligence reasons, or could it merely be that he wanted to sell it to the highest bidder? Whatever the reason, he would be here in less than two days. Vollen would have to act fast to protect Ran.

Another piece of information on the screen made Vollen's heart race: Buchner was always accompanied by a terminator. Trained as assassins, terminators were genetically enhanced athletes with keen abilities. They were highly dangerous persons, totally devoid of feeling. Some had been known to strangle their mothers on command.

An intrusion signal beeped. Someone was at the door. Flipping on the monitor, Vollen saw Sheeb standing outside. Vollen put on his shirt and half-buttoned it as he walked to the door. The door slid open, and Vollen motioned Sheeb into the room. "So what's up?" Vollen asked, the door closing behind him.

"Plenty." Sheeb walked over to one of the small sofas and sat down. "I've made contact with Ran."

"You what?" Vollen asked incredulously.

"Made contact." Sheeb seemed perplexed by Vollen's reaction.

"But I didn't see anything in the monitor."

"So that was you moving the camera. I wanted to smash it."

"It's my job, Sheeb. But I don't understand how you....."

"Telepathy...We talked telepathically."

Vollen's eyes dilated slightly and he looked up at the corner of the room for a moment. He turned his gaze back to Sheeb. "So what did you find out?"

"He's in some kind of neurological state I've never seen before. His brain is pumping endorphins like it's the end of the universe. The guy is stoned out of his mind."

Vollen laughed. "So that explains why he sits and looks at orchids all day."

"Exactly."

"So what about the Mind War Machine?" Vollen asked as he pulled up one of the chairs and sat down.

"I haven't gotten that far yet."

"Well, I suggest you hurry up, because we've got a problem on our hands."

"What problem?"

"That accident we had on Alpha Lyra wasn't an accident. It was planned by a guy named Charles Buchner, and Darkos is in with him."

Sheeb raised a hand to his chin and stared across the room. "That's not all." Sheeb turned and looked at Vollen.

"Buchner is headed here within forty-eight hours. We've got to get out of here."

"What do you suggest?" Sheeb asked.

"I think we should go to Darkos and give her some kind of story about needing to move Ran to the guest cottage with you. After we transfer Ran, I'll see about stealing one of the transports."

"What kind of story?" Sheeb asked.

"You're the expert. Concoct something." Vollen got up and walked over to the terminal. Shutting down the screen, he had the oddest feeling, as if he were still inside his dream.

"All right, I've got it." Sheeb said.

"Good, let's go."

Vollen walked over to the door and as it slid open, Sheeb followed him into the hallway. As the door shut, Vollen activated the security system. The walk to the elevator and the ride down to Darkos's office was spent in silence, each man alone with himself.

Vollen was still partly in his dream world of dying quasars. He could feel the icy touch of the Dark Mother and the spiraling galaxies that made up her body. The feeling of annihilation struck him with dread, and yet in some strange way he yearned for it.

Sheeb's thoughts went to Ran, upstairs in the solarium. He couldn't shake off the feelings he had felt in Ran's presence. They reminded him of his experience with the dolphins back on Christos. But what did they mean? Surely they were only the result of a destabilization of brain chemistry. Probably a jump in the perceptive neurotransmitter levels. How else could one explain the sudden awesome beauty of the world that had been laid out before Sheeb's eyes, when only moments before everything had been normal? In reality, Sheeb assured himself, things don't shimmer with light. But in those few moments before Sheeb had forced himself out of it, the world had seemed perfect. Time had disappeared, and in that pulsing beautiful moment he and Ran were together once again.

So which is real, Sheeb asked himself—the indescribable peace of those moments with Ran, or the stalking danger of Darkos? One thing was certain. If Sheeb didn't deal with the grotesque reality of Darkos, Ran would have no brain to experience his rapture with. The Deep Mind Probes would see to that.

The hallway opened into the oval reception area. Vollen walked over to the receptionist, Sheeb following close behind.

"Hello, Barbara."

The brunette receptionist looked up and smiled. "Oh, 'tis Alex!"

"Would you tell Darkos that Alan Sheeb and I are here?"

"Sure will." The attractive woman reached over for the intercom. "I'd do anything for you, Alex." Her eyelids fluttered like mascaraed moths, just barely noticeable, and thus all the more alluring.

Darkos answered the intercom. "Yes?"

"Mr. Vollen and Dr. Sheeb are here to see you."

"Send them in."

Vollen and Sheeb headed for the door to Darkos's office. Darkos was sitting behind her desk, and motioned the two men to sit down. The giant lizard was sleeping, its abdomen swelling with each inhale.

"So, gentlemen, do you have anything for me?"

"As a matter of fact, I do." Sheeb said.

"Go on," Darkos said.

"I've completed my preliminary assessment of Dr. Farr, and I have determined that he is suffering from a severe psychotic break. He is, quite frankly, not in the same reality as you or I. I don't detect any organic damage, but he is very disoriented." Sheeb paused and looked Darkos directly in the eyes. "I would like to take Dr. Farr back to the guest cottage and work with him in more comfortable surroundings. I feel that a dramatic change in environment would help our task considerably."

Darkos leaned back in her chair, obviously displeased. "I'm afraid that's impossible."

"I'm afraid that unless we do this, we may never get Dr. Farr to come around." Sheeb said.

"I can't authorize this, Dr. Sheeb. There is a distressing lack of security at the cottage."

There was an awkward silence in the room as Darkos and Sheeb looked at each other. Vollen broke it. "If you can't, I will."

Darkos turned and looked at Vollen as a predator looks at its prey.

Vollen continued. "I was hoping to have your cooperation in this, Ms. Darkos, but I really don't need it."

"What do you mean?" Darkos's words bristled.

"I mean that I am the Information Security Officer on this project, and as such, Dr. Farr is under my jurisdiction, not yours. And if you insist on this position, I will simply call Alfred Bach in Bethesda and get his authorization to move Dr. Farr."

He was right. Darkos had received word from Bach that Vollen had top authority in the Farr affair. "As you wish." The thin veneer of Darkos's civility barely concealed her seething rage. She casually reached for a tumbler of water, an act that might have conveyed an air of unconcern had her hand not trembled. "I'll notify Dr. Hoffman that he's to give Dr. Farr his daily vitamin injections at the guest cottage."

Darkos made a note in her personal calendar as if to remind herself, though in reality she had written nothing. Her right hand, trembling with rage, had scribbled a circular whirl of black ink. "Anything else, gentlemen?" Darkos asked.

"Not at the moment, no." Vollen rose from his chair.

Darkos motioned toward the door as she took another sip of water from her glass. She watched Vollen and Sheeb leave, and sat there for the longest time just staring at the door. Finally, setting the glass of water back on her desk, she called Hoffman and told him to push the distillation process as much as possible. He could cut maybe ten or so hours off the time, but to do it faster would be dangerous.

Darkos rose from her chair and paced the room, cursing to herself. She felt something stirring inside of her. She did not know how, but she would make Vollen pay for this. She picked up a memo pad from her desk and threw it across the room. It struck the edge of the terrarium and the giant lizard jerked itself out of deep sleep. It hissed into the air, and its feet clawed the earth as it turned around on itself looking for the intruder. One open eye watched its captor across the room. For a moment, Darkos thought she saw the look of hatred in the reptilian eye. And then it closed, leaving Darkos with the realization that the feeling of hatred belonged not to the reptile, but to her.

CHAPTER TWENTY-THREE

Vollen and Sheeb guided a glassy-eyed Ran toward the guest cottage and the small windswept cropping of trees that surrounded it. Ran's eyes, still unfocused, sat transfixed by some inner world. His condition reminded Sheeb of pictures he had seen of the Indian saint Ramakrishna. The nineteenth century mystic had gone so deeply into samadhi, a kind of inner bliss, that he had to be carried around by his disciples. Unattended, he had been known to fall flat on his face utterly unaware of his body and still deep in ecstasy.

To have glimpsed Ran's world had been a terrible and beautiful thing. It had shaken Sheeb, to his very core, and even now, walking toward the cottage, he was reluctant to drop into sync with him again.

The golden orb of the sun was quickly slipping beneath the sea. Off on the horizon, billows of orange and magenta burst into flame. With each breath, it seemed, the stars overhead became more distinct as the last dying light of day quickly turned an azure blue. In that exquisite moment of beauty Sheeb smiled. For no apparent reason, his mind recalled an odd bit of trivia—the sun was not setting at all. In fact what men called sunrise and sunset did not actually exist. It was only from the limited terrestrial view that such an event occurred. In truth it was the Earth's rotation that created the illusion, not the Sun. What appears to be, is not always the truth.

Perhaps it was the thought about the illusion of sunset that fired the holomemory within his mind. But suddenly Sheeb was back in the fifth grade. It was a spring day. Everyone had been given new textbooks and the smell of new paper and fresh ink filled the air. His book lay open on his desk, the crisp pages having just been turned to the chapter on Copernicus. Sister Theresa had just written the astronomer's name on the chalkboard when the class broke into stifled giggles. Unknown to the nun, a piece of white toilet paper from her venture into the restroom was clinging to the back of her black habit. The lone tissue clung against her habit just as stubbornly as the Church of Rome had clung to the old worldview that Earth was the center of the solar system. Copernicus's heresy was to have shock-waved a civilization with the notion that Earth was not the center, nor man. He had stolen the center stage of the cosmos from the earth and had given to the Sun, an act that would cost him dearly.

Centauri barked, and Sheeb was roused from his reveries. Vollen had thrown a stick into the air, and looked over at Sheeb and smiled as the dog leapt into the air to catch it in his mouth. And yes, Vollen had watched the monitors intently and missed everything. The outer reality had cast its net of illusion and Vollen had seen nothing, for there had been nothing to see. The events unfolding between Sheeb and Ran had taken place in an altogether different realm, but what realm—the world of dream? Could such things have really happened? Had Ran entered another reality or was he just a madman seducing Sheeb into a dangerous world?

"Don't be so paranoid!" Ran spoke silently from somewhere in Sheeb's mind.

"What do you mean, don't be so paranoid?" Sheeb spoke back telepathically.

Vollen continued walking, completely unaware of the conversation taking place between Sheeb and Ran.

"From over here," Sheeb continued, "your behavior looks very strange."

"And from over here" Ran offered, "your perceptions look very limited."

"Limited?"

"Yes, Sheeb, limited. That dangerous world you are so afraid of is the most exquisitely beautiful universe you could ever imagine."

"But is it real?" Sheeb asked.

"Real?" The air was broken by Ran's laughter as he collapsed to the ground.

"He's done this twice before," Vollen offered. "It seems to come for no apparent reason."

Vollen and Sheeb watched as Ran continued howling, until finally his noises softened and turned to slight moans of pleasure. He had slipped his hand up under his shirt and was stroking his belly as he gazed upward and into the sky.

"Shall we?" Vollen reached down as if ready to lift Ran up. Sheeb nodded. A hand under each shoulder, they lifted Ran onto his feet and continued on the narrow path to the cottage. Sheeb dropped into sync again, but Ran was nowhere to be found. Wherever he had gone, Sheeb was unable to follow.

Arriving at the cottage, Vollen and Sheeb guided their charge into the living room and sat him down in one of the large overstuffed chairs. After making sure everything was in order, Vollen left for the parking garage to see about stealing one of the transports. Sheeb followed him to the door. "Be careful," Sheeb said and lightly touched Vollen on the shoulder. Vollen looked at him for a moment and then disappeared into the silvery dimness of starlight.

Stepping outside, Sheeb walked to the deck that overlooked the sea. The last vestiges of sunlight had dissolved on the far horizon. The great sun was now gone, and the air was turning cold as galaxies of molecular oxygen cooled down. Staring off into space, Sheeb had the sudden and unexpected image of Darkos and her pet lizard. He shook the image from his mind, not knowing that he had somehow actually tuned into Darkos, not knowing that his contact with Ran was stimulating latent psychic powers.

Ellen Darkos had retrieved another small tree frog from her collection box and slipped it into the terrarium with the sleeping reptile. Upon seeing the massive monster, the tiny frog jumped hysterically, making barely audible screeches. The lizard opened an eye and watched the frog bumping into its glass wall. Satiated and disinterested, the lizard looked at the amphibian for a moment and then closed its leathery eyelids and returned to sleep.

Sometimes Darkos would make the reptile wait for his food, wait until it was mad with hunger. It was then that she liked to watch the feeding, for it was at these times that the creature's vicious cruelty was at its zenith. It could jump the entire length of its terrarium, some fifteen feet, to break the back of a hamster. But now, for some reason, Darkos didn't feel like tormenting the thing. Perhaps it was because she felt the limits of her own invisible cage.

Picking up a pencil and beside herself with anxiety, she paced back and forth, rearranging magazines on the two office tables. Within hours she would have the synthesized Demerol 57, but what if Sheeb were able to wrestle the information for the Mind War Machine from

Ran before Hoffman injected the memory suppressant? Perhaps Buchner was right. Perhaps she should have killed Sheeb. A wave of anger swept over her and she swallowed the feeling, tasting the gall of it. Unknown to her, the act of swallowing her anger had set off a series of neurotransmitter events in her brain. Fueled by the protein snack of sushi she had eaten earlier (the fish was alive only moments before being served), the freed adrenaline of her anger was shifting the subtle balance within her hypothalamus. Inexplicably, Darkos felt the sudden stirrings of sexual desire. At first it was just a fantasy of Jeff's hard cock down her throat, and then she felt it. She could almost taste it. In the alchemy of her brain it didn't matter. If she would not allow herself to feel her burning anger, the deep limbic brain would transmute it into sexual desire. Either way, it would vent the pressure. Darkos sighed and crossed the room toward her desk. Her left hand glided over the fake veneer surface to the waiting intercom, the shape of which struck Ellen as oddly erotic.

"Yes?" The young motor pool employee who had picked up Sheeb and Vollen answered.

"Jeff, this is Ellen Darkos."

"Yes, ma'am?"

"I'd like to talk with you, if I might."

"Ok, I'll be right up."

"No, Jeff." Darkos ran her fingers through a wisp of hair at her temple. "I'll meet you in your quarters."

"Will this, uh, meeting involve anything other than talking?" he asked.

"Why do you ask?" Darkos's voice sounded amused.

"It's just I'm dirty and wonder if I should take a shower."

"Jeff."

"Yes?"

"Take a shower."

Darkos hung up and slowly pulled a hair clip through her hair. Gazing across the room, she thought about raising Jeff to an office position. That way he'd be closer. It was such a long walk to his quarters by the transport area. But what on earth would he do? The boy was totally useless. The only thing he was good for was fucking.

Darkos grabbed her purse and walked from the office. Her fingers opened the clasp to her alligator handbag and searched for the comforting metallic feel of her pulse laser. It had settled down to the bottom of her purse next to a couple of pastel tissues. As her fingers ruffled through the contents, she closed the door to her office and headed toward the motor pool. A slight smile of pleasure came across her lips as Darkos found the deadly electronics. It was simply pragmatic. For her, the world was a dangerous place. No one was safe; no one could be trusted. And this truth was strangely comforting to the woman now poised between rage and desire.

CHAPTER TWENTY-FOUR

Vollen could barely make out Sheeb's silhouette against the doorway to the cottage. Above, a quilt of stars blanketed itself across the blackness of night. The narrow path, winding its way through a sea of dead grass, seemed to Vollen like some dark serpent crawling its way toward the Bosk mansion. The main building lay ten minutes away.

The sound of the ocean rolled through the starlit darkness, and the heady aroma of sea breeze filled the air. Vollen breathed in deeply, letting the sweetness of the odor surround him. The smell of ocean breeze and the sight of stars filled his senses.

Gazing upward at the heavens, Vollen felt suddenly very alone. Up there, without the thin cushion of air surrounding earth, all life would perish. Only the anaerobic bacteria might survive until the frigid womb of eternal night crystallized them into electronic ice. Where was comfort in a universe such as this?

Vollen rubbed his shoulder where Sheeb had touched him only moments before. Something in him was awakening, a numbing sleep was coming to an end. Sensing his response to Sheeb's touch, Vollen chastised himself yet again. Comfort, he reasoned, was not in something as innocuous as kindness, nor in its handmaiden, a gentle touch. It lay in knowing what you had to do and in knowing that you would do it, no matter what.

The Bosk mansion suddenly loomed up before him like the ghost of a monster. Rising up from the earth, the white concrete walls seemed to pulsate in the dim starlight. The transport area lay on the far side of the building, perhaps another five minutes. Vollen inched his way around the back of the building as stars drifted toward the horizon in silence. The aroma of the ocean suddenly mixed with the freshwater smell of Weirman Lake. Here and there a few bullfrogs sang their nightly mating songs, and the stars above were reflected on the glass-like surface of the water.

———————————————

Jeff had propped himself in bed against some pillows. Beads of water on his naked chest and thighs were evaporating in the cool air of the bedroom. His right hand held a Hard Lick to his mouth as he listened to the pulsing sounds of the Vulvonics. Hard Licks were Jeff's favorite candy. Made from a hard chocolate, the confections were shaped like tongues and put on a stick. They had been the rage for the last six months, and the Vulvonics' fame had increased as a result. They were featured on every wrapper. Jeff let the sweetness of the Lick drip onto his tongue as another kind of sweetness stirred from his pelvis.

There was a knock at the door. Jeff rolled over and turned down the stereo. The Vulvonics' pulsing rhythm was reduced to a whisper. "It's open, come in." Jeff threw the corner of his towel over his hardening cock. He folded the towel back just enough to reveal a line of dark pubic hair. He loved baiting Darkos.

Darkos walked in and closed the door behind her. Her eye caught the Hard Lick wrapper on the floor beside the bed. The Vulvonics' Merissa stared up at her, a whip in one hand, a trident in another. Darkos reached down and picked it up.

"You're such a slob."

Jeff shrugged and put out his hand for the wrapper. Darkos passed it to him, and he rolled over to toss it into the trash. Exaggerating the move, Jeff pulled his thigh slightly forward to let his cock slide part way into view.

Darkos felt her knees weaken. The buttons wouldn't come undone fast enough. "Fuck it," she thought as she ripped the last button off and pulled the blouse from her shoulders. By the time Jeff rolled back around, Darkos was naked.

Sliding his hand down his right thigh, Jeff pulled his engorged organ onto his hard belly and spread his legs, yawning and stretching. His hands grabbed a pillow and pulled it down onto his chest. He would need something soft to hold onto. Darkos was so hard, every sinew in her body sprung like steel coils.

Without so much as a word, Darkos slid onto the sheets. Slipping her hands under his buttocks, she pulled him back to her and slid his hard cock into the hot cavern of her mouth. With each thrust Darkos pulled him deeper and deeper into her throat. As the head of his sex pushed open the back of her throat, the muscles of her esophagus relaxed and the scream that had lodged itself in her throat began to lessen. Darkos arched her head back pulling the serpent forward and dragging Jeff even closer.

Jeff's body began to quiver from so much sensation so fast. He let go of the pillow and clawed the sheets as a volcano within him began to stir. Jeff's moans and Darkos's breathing were broken by a loud noise in the corner of the room.

"Shit," Jeff yelled.

"What was that?" Darkos let go of Jeff's cock and it fell with a thud onto his stomach.

"It's the automatic monitor," Jeff's voice strained with frustration.

"What alarm?" Darkos asked. "The primary security system?"

"No, it's a silicon chip camera I connected to my computer monitor. I just installed it in the garage a couple of days ago."

"So what is it monitoring?" Darkos asked impatiently.

"The transport area. It sits on the south wall of the service bay."

"I don't like my personnel installing anything I don't know about." Darkos motioned toward the computer in the corner of the room. "Turn it on."

Jeff jumped from bed, walked over to the screen, and flipped a switch. The monitor flashed on and Darkos watched an image of Vollen slinking across the parking area into one of the large garages.

Vollen had disarmed the central monitoring system, but was unaware of the second. Easing himself up against the side of one of the transports, Vollen looked around to see if there was anyone in the area. Unlikely at three in the morning, but you never knew.

The transports were tethered via cable to various generators, which hummed as they sent energy into the batteries that serviced the electric motors. Vollen checked the instrument panel on one of the transports: two-thirds to capacity. The next one over was fully charged. He was reaching down and disconnecting the transport from its umbilicus when a door opened.

"So what have we here, an early morning ride?" Darkos's voice chilled with innuendo.

Vollen said nothing. He just looked at her and the pulse laser in her hand.

"It looks to me like you were preparing to steal that transport." Darkos cocked her head to one side. "You'd better have one hell of an explanation."

Vollen cleared his throat. "We thought we'd take Ran for a joyride, maybe loosen him up some."

"Without a motor pool authorization? Sure." Darkos turned to Jeff. "Step outside."

"Excuse me?" he asked.

Darkos yelled, the walls of the garage echoing back her rage. "I said, step outside!"

Jeff turned and walked through one of the open doors. Darkos pointed the laser at Vollen and smiled. In a moment of disturbing silence, she looked him over and aimed the small device at his gut. Her eyelids closed slightly, and as her eyes slid up into her head with pleasure, a strange smile etched itself across her face. She pulled the trigger and the air snapped as the white searing shaft of light cut a path to Vollen.

As the screaming mass of photons sliced into his belly, the flash of heat spread like a smelting furnace through his trunk up to his throat and out his limbs. It all happened in a few nanoseconds. Vollen never realized what had happened. The sudden flush of heat drove him delirious in the fraction of a second before vaporization. As the heat hit his brain, the water inside every cell boiled. The seething cloud of steam cracked open his skull just as his skeleton began to ionize.

There was a sudden swoosh as his entire body vaporized into a cloud of agonized steam and ionizing gas. The swirling cloud of gases tornadoed up to the ceiling, and eddied themselves against the rafters. As the coolness of the metal roof calmed down the rioting molecules, some of the gas condensed back into bodily fluids. A thin circle of lipids dripped from the ceiling to the concrete floor below.

Darkos sauntered over to the small puddle and slid her shoe through what was left of Alex Vollen. She threw back her head and laughed. Turning to the open door, Darkos called Jeff back into the garage. As he entered she handed him a mop that had been leaning up against the windowsill.

"Here, mop that up." Darkos pointed to the liquid remains of Vollen, "and forget what you saw. You were with me in a conference—do you understand?"

"Yes, ma'am." Jeff nodded and wrapped his arms around his shivering body.

Darkos checked her watch. Within an hour or so the Memerol would be ready. Ran's mind would be in her possession, and not even Sheeb would be able to wrestle it from her. She stepped outside. The horizon was turning gray as the sun began its easterly approach. Breathing deeply, Darkos drew in the fragrant air. It was to be a glorious day, an absolutely glorious day.

CHAPTER TWENTY-FIVE

It happened in the split second before the searing blade of light had sliced into Vollen's gut, with Darkos watching as his flesh vaporized into eddies of gas and drops of fat. She would remember with relish the screaming sound of his death. But she had not seen him moving beyond it. No one had.

Vollen was catapulting back-ward. Even before the laser hit him, he knew something strange had happened. He watched himself getting smaller as he was thrown up against the ceiling. And as he felt himself pass through the roof, he saw his body below exploding into a writhing mass of steam and shredded electrons.

Everything accelerated. An awe-some force was pulling Vollen into a tunnel of light. But what? How could this be? His body was gone. Suddenly, without knowing how, Vollen felt an awareness growing inside of him. It was as if he were expanding into everywhere at once.

Images of Sheeb standing by the cottage rushed through him...a shooting star fell into the dark sea.... Ran sitting alone, staring at the carpet, immersed in bliss. Vollen felt drawn into Ran's mysterious world. Ran turned and smiled at him, and for the first time in Vollen's life he saw and felt the world to be a beautiful place, scintillating with a rare and luminous beauty. But it only lasted a moment, for Vollen felt the strange power propelling him deeper into the tunnel.

Whales were swimming off the coastline, heading for the Arctic, and in that instant, Vollen knew their thoughts. In another moment he felt everything on the planet, all the lives, all the dreams, all the desires. The power of the perception tidal-waved through him like a cosmic tsunami. His edges were dissolving, and he screamed from the intensity. But he had no voice. There was only silence.

The light of the tunnel turned diamond white, and Vollen passed out. There was a swooshing sound as the tunnel turned in on itself. And in a final flash of light, the last boundaries between Vollen and the world were sheared away.

CHAPTER TWENTY-SIX

Kathrina fed another piece of dry wood to the fire she had been tending for half the night. Shadows danced about her as amber flames licked the cool air, and the moon, a disc of molten silver, glided soundlessly through a starry night.

Normally Kathrina conducted the sacred fire ceremony when the moon was full and sometimes when it was new or a mere crescent in the sky. Tonight, however, the full moon was two days away. But something inside had been tugging at her, something gnawing at her ever since Remeira had left. Kathrina hoped that tending the sacred flames would purify her and leave her with a heightened understanding and insight, as it so often had before.

The breezes drifting in from the ocean were cooler than usual, and Kathrina pulled her shawl closely about her shoulders. Reaching into her basket of offerings, Kathrina pinched a handful of rice with the thumb and second finger of her right hand as she began to chant, "Om Namaha Shivaya."

Then she tossed the few grains of rice to the hungry flame. The chant, ancient and primordial, was in honor of Shiva, Lord of the Universe. Her hand reached into the basket for more rice as she gazed into the red-hot embers. Breathing deeply, she relished the aromas of the burning wood, rice, and incense.

She chanted again, but this time she invoked the name of the ancient goddess Kali, dark Mother of the Universe: "Om Kali Durga Namo Nama."

Again she held the grains of rice between her thumb and second finger. Her index finger pointed outward, useless to the task of holding the rice. This gesture, handed down for aeons, spoke eloquently though silently about man's relationship to the divine. The index finger, associated with the ego, was not used in offerings to the sacred fire, for only by transcending or perhaps transmuting the ego was it possible for man or woman to approach divinity.

Kathrina looked at her hand and, sighing, reached back into the basket, this time pulling out a freshly cut flower. Again she chanted the name of the dark goddess: "Om Kali Durga Namo Nama." The flames kissed the moist petals of the rose as droplets of water sizzled in the heat and the aroma of roses filled the air.

The smell of roses carried Kathrina's mind back to Remeira, for her cherished student had often put roses in her hair, braiding them into her dreadlocks. The thought of her brought a great sadness to Kathrina's heart. They had worked together side by side for seven years, and now Remeira was gone. It had seemed like a dream, her leaving. Only hours before, she had stood on the verandah looking out to the sea with Kathrina. In her hands Remeira had held a coconut, the air pregnant with the smell of oranges ripening on dwarf tress that huddled in next to the cottage.

"It is time for me to go, Kathrina."

"What do you mean?" Kathrina asked.

"I'm going back to Kings Port."

186

"What on earth for, Remeira, what about our work together?" There was a sudden urgency in Kathrina's voice.

"Shhh…" Remeira put a finger to her lips. "My destiny calls me. I have no choice." Remeira looked Kathrina in the eyes. "You have given me so much, Kathrina. I can never repay you."

"I never expected you to pay anything, and you know it."

"Kathrina, our time together has passed. You cannot teach me anymore." Remeira's eyes looked to the floor for a moment, and then looked back up. "You cannot give what you do not have."

"What are you talking about, Remeira?'

"The goddess… I am talking about the goddess."

"What about her?" Kathrina asked.

Remeira took the coconut and pressed it into Kathrina's hands.

"I don't understand," Kathrina said, reluctantly taking the coconut.

"You insist on separating yourself from the goddess as if you and she were not one and the same."

Kathrina protested. "But, Remeira, I don't have the powers that Luna has. I don't even have a say about when and how Luna comes to me."

"Oh, but you do," Remeira responded. "It's just that you won't let yourself know how you do it." Remeira and Kathrina were stopped for a moment by a flash of lightning that lit up the horizon. Remeira continued. "I give you this coconut with greatest gratitude for what you have given me and with deepest sadness for what you will not give yourself."

Remeira then kissed Kathrina on the forehead, turned, and left. Down by the shoreline, she got into a small skiff and sailed out into the moonlit night for one of the neighboring islands.

Kathrina watched as the tiny boat caught the wind and pressed across silver waters. For the longest time she just stood there on the verandah looking at the empty sea and wondering if she would ever see Remeira again. The shock of the loss caused Kathrina to turn inward. The gift of the coconut was a most poignant message, for it held a metaphor, vast and ancient.

When Kathrina had first accepted Remeira as a student, Kathrina had given her a coconut, explaining that it was a primordial symbol of the ego. Like the coconut, the ego had a hard and bitter husk; like the ego, too, the coconut held within itself a sweet nectar, a nourishing food and the secret to life. Following the ego would only lead to bitterness and disillusionment. If one were to be a true vessel, if one were to be able to channel the healing stream of the Divine's love, then one had to purify oneself of ego as much as humanly possible. For Kathrina the journey of healer was also the journey of the soul, the mystic path back to the vast and mysterious source of all that was, is, and ever shall be. As with the coconut, it was only when the ego gave way and allowed the force of life within to push outward would new life begin. Otherwise, the tender shoots of growth would remain trapped inside the unyielding shell. By giving Kathrina a coconut, Remeira was telling her in a most gracious, poetic, and gentle way that the problem Kathrina faced was with her ego. How ironic if this should truly be the case.

Kathrina turned her attention back to the burning flames before her. There, under red hot embers and gray ash, she could make out one side of the coconut.

"Kali Durga Namo Nama." Kathrina began to chant the low guttural chant of Kali, the Destroyer. By invoking the destructive aspect of the goddess, she was beseeching Kali to destroy her own ignorance. If Remeira was right, she wanted to know it; she needed to know it.

"Kali Durga Namo Nama." As if on cue, thick smoke began to swirl about her as a cold wind swept in from the sea. Shards of cloud floated across the moon like broken pieces of pottery and then the world was once again bathed in silver light.

Kathrina began the Breath of Fire, the bellows of her lungs filling her with pranic force. She gasped. The goddess was in front of her. Hovering above the fire pit, flame and smoke exploding all around her, Kali looked into her chela with eyes black as darkest night. Each of her hundred arms swayed in a silent dance, and every hand held a knife. In one of her left hands, she held a skull, announcing to all that she was the bringer of death to ignorance.

Kathrina looked up, her heart filled with gratitude. "Thank you," she said. The goddess looked down and snapped her fingers. Kathrina swooned. A tunnel of light opened up before her and carried her away. No longer earthbound, her mind soared through dimensions of light and sound, soft pinks, swirling purples and streams of gold. The sound of sea conchs and wind chimes filled her head.

And then, as if from outer space, she saw the Earth floating in a sea of stars. Swooping down like a falcon from the heavens, Kathrina gasped as all of Earth passed through her. Ponies pranced in autumn meadows as crickets sang their last symphonies, and leaves turned brown and brittle as trees pulled their sap deep into the earth for winter's sleep. Still the images tidal-waved through her, whales heading north to the waters off Vancouver, farmers gathering their wheat in the fields of Kansas. She panicked. Where was she? She was everywhere, stretched as it were like some vast canvas across the surface of the entire planet. She felt herself giving birth to a thousand infants, her body the bodies of all mothers. She felt them, each and every child, suckling at her breasts. She felt their mothers' relief at birth completed, and she felt their mothers' dreams for what their children might become. Her body quivered as she felt the omnipresent web of life, the birthing and the dying of a million forms, human and animal, microscopic and leviathan.

And then the vision snapped. Her awareness was no longer stretched across the Earth, but hovered in the back alley of some Manhattan street. It was night, and all was dark save the flash of steel as a robber brandished his knife. A startled youth backed up against a chain-link fence as the mugger grabbed his sweatshirt and pulled it up around the young man's throat. He jabbed the serrated blade into the smooth flesh of his victim's belly. The young boy-man gasped in horror. A cruel smile slid across the murderer's lips as he sliced deep and pulled the blade out sideways. Anguished cries echoed off soot-covered brick walls as his victim's paralyzed body slid to the ground.

The robber quickly rifled through the young man's jeans searching for cash as a torrent of blood pulsed from torn arteries. Having collected all of twenty dollars, the murderous thief ran off into the shadows as a gentle rain began to fall across the city. Kathrina pulled herself from the distasteful vision only to see the goddess in her wrathful form staring back at her.

"You left your vigil," she said.

"I couldn't bear to watch it any longer," Kathrina said through her tears.

"My dearest chela..." There was mockery in her voice. "Until you can love the murderers as the great stream loves you, you will not be free."

"But how can I love someone who killed such an innocent one?" Kathrina yelled.

"You only love when it is convenient, and that, my dear, is not love. Your difficulty in keeping your vigil was because you refused to extend your love to someone you disliked. It is a very human trait, granted, but it is one you are expected to rise above."

Kathrina started to say something, but the goddess waved her silent.

"You live at the edge of things. You will not enter them fully, and until you do, you will not know the meaning of love." As instantly as she had appeared, she was gone.

Kathrina opened her eyes, trying to focus them in the dim light. The fire had died down to a low-lying landscape of red embers. Still entranced, she watched the dying fire for the longest time until the last hint of heat was gone. Taking a deep breath, Kathrina looked up. The moon had cut a swath across the sky to the far horizon. Hours had passed. Soon the first rays of sunlight would be dimly lighting the eastern sky.

Kathrina sighed. Remeira had been right. The problem was her ego. Even after years of teaching and healing, she could not surrender to the Divine Mother. She could not bear the tension of experiencing all of Earth's life even though to do so would be to become the goddess herself. She was not ready to let go. She needed the hard coconut.

Taking a deep breath, Kathrina looked across the ocean. At that moment she had the odd sensation of standing next to Sheeb looking out across a silent sea. A lone meteor streaked across the dark sky, and she knew, though she did not know how she knew, that Sheeb was in deathly danger.

The cold air seemed colder, and Kathrina pulled her shawl about her as she looked at the fire pit. The coconut sat there half-covered in gray ash. The fire had not yet split it. Picking it up, Kathrina pulled the large seed to her breasts, tears streaming from her eyes. As she rocked forward and backward, she gently held the warm coconut in her arms as a mother might hold a small and frightened child.

CHAPTER TWENTY-SEVEN

Sheeb stood at the deck railing, staring off into the still darkness of the sea. Only the sound of the waves and the occasional aroma of salty brine hinted at the ocean below. There was a flash of light. Looking off to the left, he caught a meteor fire-balling its way across the dark cobalt of night sky. The falling star burst into flame and fell into the sea as the Earth's atmosphere ionized the celestial visitor into burning gas.

Looking out to the distant horizon where the meteor had disappeared, Sheeb had a sudden and ominous feeling about Vollen. Had he found the transport? Would they be able to get Ran out of here? The cool breeze blowing inland suddenly seemed colder, and Sheeb pulled his jacket shut. Feeling someone behind him, he turned around to see a luminous figure.

Ran had come out of the cottage and was standing stark naked. His shoulders, arms, and thighs glowed in the faint starlight.

"Aren't you cold?" Sheeb asked telepathically.

Ran took a deep breath and walked over to the railing next to Sheeb. "No," he answered, and again, the reply seemed to come from somewhere in Sheeb's own mind.

"It's a beautiful night, isn't it?" Sheeb asked.

"It's always beautiful." Ran looked up. The cover of night sparkled with thousands of stars, most of them white with a few scattered reds and yellows. Sheeb hadn't noticed it before, but the blanket of stars seemed to be undulating. In fact, the railing, the deck, even Sheeb and Ran now seemed to be pulsating.

"He's affecting me again," Sheeb thought to himself.

"I don't know why you're so surprised. You know everything is energy. Weren't you the one who aced Quantum Mechanics 101?"

"Yes," Sheeb replied, "but it's physiologically impossible to see energy."

"Then how do you explain the fact that you are seeing it?" Ran asked.

"I assume it's a hallucination brought on, no doubt, by my being in close proximity to you." The silence was broken by Ran's sigh. He looked at Sheeb, but continued to speak telepathically.

"I know it's hard to accept. I had a hell of a time with it myself." Ran turned and looked back out to sea. "Do you know about the sea turtles here?" Ran asked.

"No."

"Well, by the late 1990s most of the sea turtles on Karpos Island were extinct, maybe a few dozen left. Some developers purchased the island for a resort and the turtles had to be moved to make way for a golf course. Richard Bosk brought them here because the climate was similar and it was a protected area."

"So where are the turtles?" Sheeb asked. "I haven't seen any."

"They're dead. They just sat on the rocks down there with their heads pulled into their shells. They sat like that for months until they all died. The shock of a new reality was too much for them to bear."

"It's a fascinating story, Ran, but there's a big difference between turtles and human beings."

"Don't flatter yourself," Ran quipped.

"Let's talk about something else."

"Pretending it's not there doesn't make it go away, Sheeb."

"Good point, Ran. Good fucking point. I couldn't agree more. So do you mind explaining how you get away with living in your world while disregarding this one?"

"Which world are you talking about?" Ran asked. "There are thousands of realities here, perhaps billions. The clams down near the waterline are experiencing this moment quite differently from you or me."

"I don't care about those clams or this epistemological bullshit. You've made agreements with Hellenstat, and now those agreements are the property of BioTech. And while you saunter around in your make-believe....excuse me...sorry... alternate reality, there are people who want the information on the Mind War Machine, and they have no qualms about how they get it."

"I'll never tell them."

"It won't matter what you want when they Deep Mind Probe you."

"We've got to make sure that no one gets this information, Sheeb. It's too dangerous."

"That's what I'm here for. Vollen is over at the transport area. When he comes back, we'll get you out of here."

"Vollen's dead."

"What?"

"Vollen is gone. I saw it."

"He what?" Sheeb asked.

"Just what I said." Ran looked at the railing sheepishly. "I know you think I'm lost in some kind of psychotic fantasy, but while I was in there I saw Darkos vaporize him over in the transport area."

Sheeb looked at Ran with surprise, not knowing if there was any truth in what had been said.

Ran looked back at him but continued to speak telepathically. "Consciousness is non-local, Sheeb. We are duped into believing that we are confined to these bodies."

"Yeah, yeah, yeah," Sheeb responded condescendingly. "That old Vedanta/Buddhist bullshit may be true. But if your brain is Deep Mind Probed it won't matter." Sheeb sighed and looked out across the dark water. "We'll wait until morning to see if Vollen comes back. If he doesn't, we'll have to come up with something."

Ran nodded toward the horizon. "Morning is not far away, Sheeb." It was true. The first faint hints of gray were wisping themselves across the eastern sky. A lone seagull, stirring itself from nocturnal sleep, rose from the rocks below and glided into the quiet air.

"How about some hot tea?" Sheeb asked.

"Sure."

Sheeb reached out his arm and draped it around Ran's shoulders. As they walked toward the door of the cottage, Sheeb looked at Ran with a perplexed expression.

"So, I don't understand why you don't talk out loud, like norm..."

"Like normal people?" Ran asked telepathically.

"Well, yes."

"At first it was shock. After I translated the cube, I saw the universe in a way I had never imagined. When I saw how I had violated the interconnectedness of things, I couldn't speak."

Sheeb opened the door to the cottage, and Ran stepped inside, continuing to talk telepathically. "But as the shock wore off and I found myself marooned in this new world, I discovered that it took too much energy to talk. I preferred silence. Besides, I found everything people talked about boring." Ran sat down at the kitchen table and started fiddling with a paper napkin.

"You used the word marooned," Sheeb noted as he pulled two cups from the shelf. "Do you mean you couldn't find a way out of your altered perception?"

"Yes, as a matter of fact. When Christopher Columbus headed for the New World, he used his navigation charts to get him to the edge of the known world. I, on the other hand, had no navigation charts. I was completely lost in a new reality I had never even imagined existed."

"So, are you comparing yourself to Christopher Columbus?" Sheeb asked.

"We both stumbled onto new worlds. I just hope I don't bring the pestilence of Western civilization into this one."

"Pestilence, Ran? That's a harsh word."

"And what word would you use, Sheeb, considering how the Europeans marched into the Americas and methodically raped and pillaged the native peoples and resources? And the result of this devastation, Sheeb, was to destroy whole cultures, which I have now come to believe hold keys to our survival as a species."

"Don't you think it's straining the metaphor a bit to think of yourself as a modern Christopher Columbus?" Sheeb poured water into the teacups and set them in the microwave. Closing the door to the oven he thought about asking Ran exactly what keys he thought the ancient Americas held for the modern world, but decided to avoid the question.

"Magellan, then," Ran retorted.

"What does Ferdinand have to do with your predicament?"

"Your predicament as well, my friend."

"Please do enlighten me," Sheeb said as he sat at the table next to Ran.

"Surely you know the story about Magellan's trip to Tierra del Fuego."

"No, I can't say that I do."

"Well, like Columbus, Magellan was an explorer. When he entered the Pacific Ocean he stopped at the tip of South America."

"Tierra del Fuego," Sheeb noted.

"Yes," Ran replied. "The expedition had a historian on board, so the encounter was written down. When Magellan came ashore, he was asked by the local natives how he got there. When he pointed to the full-masted sailing ships at anchor, they couldn't see anything. They had never seen such things, never imagined such things, and so they filtered them out of their perception. Finally someone in the tribe saw the ships, and said that if you looked out of the corner of your eye, you could see something. That person, Sheeb, was the village shaman."

"Are you claiming to be some kind of modern shaman?" Sheeb asked.

"I'm only saying that there are things we never see because we never imagine them. We live in a land-locked world of hardened perception. We think we know what reality is. But we are only living on the veneer. The depths terrify us, and if we were ever to experience reality directly, we would lose our minds."

"Is that what happened to you?"

"Sort of... I had to lose my mind to find myself."

"I won't even begin to respond to that one," Sheeb said.

The bell to the microwave went off. Sheeb pulled out the mugs and slipped tea bags into the two steaming cups. Setting them on the table, he scooted one over to Ran. They drank their tea silently for a moment, the fragrance of oranges and spice filling the air.

"I have a question." Sheeb broke the mental silence.

"Yes?" Ran looked over at Sheeb.

"Why did you walk out after Susan died?"

Ran ran a finger over the edges of his napkin as if trying to smooth it out.

"You weren't even at the funeral," Sheeb said.

199

"I can't."

"What do you mean, you can't?"

"Sheeb, I've spent ten years trying to forget."

"So have I! But if you can pawn your new world off on me, then you can at least know how it feels in mine. And it hurts over here."

Ran looked across the room at an imaginary spot on the wall. His eyes seemed transfixed, and Sheeb had the sudden impression that he was alone in the kitchen. The leviathan of sadness arched its back again, and Sheeb felt suddenly very alone and very small, as if the universe had collapsed in on him. He reached over for his tea when he caught an eddy of pheromones coming from Ran. A series of holomemories fired in his brain with such explosive force that it almost knocked him on the floor. They poured through his mind like a torrent. Every smile, every touch, every laugh with Ran echoed through Sheeb's mind. "Fuck you!" Sheeb yelled. He grabbed Ran's mug and tossed the hot tea on his chest. He wasn't about to let his friend disappear again without a fight.

Ran screamed, the sound of his agonized voice bouncing off the walls of the kitchen. Sheeb jumped across the room and filled a glass with cold water and tossed it on Ran's chest. The water dripped down the front of his body, his sides, the chair, and onto the floor.

"Why did you do that?" Ran bellowed. His fist pounded the table with such force, the mugs jumped.

"Oh, so you can talk!" Sheeb replied casually.

"I don't understand why you did that to me."

Sheeb looked Ran straight in the eyes. "You left me once. I just got pissed that you bolted again."

Ran's expression softened as he dried himself off with a kitchen towel lying on the table. "I'm sorry. It's just too painful." He had returned to his telepathic communication.

"Ran, there may be a billion other realities at this moment, but one of those realities is that both of us are still hurting. It's like you said—pretending that something isn't there doesn't make it go away."

Ran wiped a tear from his eye and placed it in the middle of the paper triangle. Sheeb continued, pretending not to notice. "You're not the only one who's spent ten years trying to forget what happened on that boat." Sheeb poured half of his tea into Ran's empty cup. "Susan's gone, Ran, and there's nothing we can do about it." Sheeb handed Ran the cup and Ran pulled it in close. The warmth felt comforting.

"I miss her too," Sheeb's voice cracked with emotion, "but we can't bring her back." Their eyes met and Sheeb reached over and touched Ran's outstretched arm. "But you're here; I'm here, and I don't want to lose you again."

There was a noise at the glass door. "Centauri!" Sheeb walked over to the door and slid it open as the animal slipped inside. The fresh air of early morning washed into the kitchen as Centauri padded his way into the room. He lowered his head to the floor and sniffed as he walked around the cabinets and back to Sheeb. The dog rubbed himself against Sheeb's legs and then sat on his haunches looking up at his master. Sheeb scratched his ears and walked back to the table. The animal followed him, and then stopped short in front of Ran. He looked up and stared into Ran's eyes. Rose-pinks and blue-greens were spiraling around Ran's head and chest. Glancing at the dog, Sheeb noticed that the colored lights were coming from Centauri's heart, just as Sheeb had seen on the deck at the Bosk mansion.

Ran seemed entranced by the energy coming off Centauri, as a stream of tears rolled down his cheeks. Sheeb broke the silence. "Vollen said that after you 'translated' the carbonite cube, you were found weeping and hugging one of the electrician's dogs."

"Yes." Ran continued to speak telepathically, as did Sheeb.

"Did this same thing happen then?"

"Sort of." Ran continued to look into Centauri's eyes as he spoke. "After the blinders were removed from my eyes, after I saw how everything is connected to everything else, how the farthest stars are woven together with the tiniest of life forms—I..." Ran stopped abruptly and stared at the floor.

Sheeb felt him slipping away, and reached out to touch his arm. "Go on," he said.

Ran shook his head. "I...just staggered out into the hall, numb from the immensity of what I had just seen. I nearly stepped on Zack, who was sitting in front of my door. He just looked up at me and wagged his tail." Ran fingered a paper napkin for a moment.

"I saw my reflection in his brown eyes, and I was filled with shame. I had just hurled a carbonite cube through the veils that separate universes from each other. I had created a rift that had never been intended. Through that one ignorant act I had cursed humanity with the distinct possibility of another techno-logical disaster. I wept for Zack. I wept for all the animals that have to suffer because of us, and I wept for us, Sheeb, all of us arrogant humans who think we know what is real and that it is ours just for the taking. Odd, isn't it, that I'd open myself to an animal that couldn't talk, but in that moment he was my most perfect confessor."

"I don't understand," Sheeb said.

"Of course you don't. You insist on seeing the old world and not the new."

CHAPTER TWENTY-SEVEN

"Just call me turtle."

"More like a tortoise, I'd say." Ran leaned back in his chair with a slight grin on his face.

"There are a few things I've been meaning to ask you." Sheeb looked at Ran expectantly.

"Go on." Ran said.

"Why did you come up with the term 'translation' for the act of sending the cube into another dimension, and why carbonite?"

"I chose carbonite because it has a great capacity for holding information, and it also resonates with the carbon-based system of our own bodies. It just facilitated the resonance required for the psychic interface."

"Makes sense," Sheeb said. "But why the word 'translation'? It's a linguistic term."

"Exactly!"

"I don't get it," Sheeb said as he took a sip of his tea.

"Everything is language, Sheeb. Just because it doesn't have words doesn't mean that it isn't language. Language conveys meaning, and the entire universe, my friend, is meaning embedded into meaning. The unimaginable beauty and the awesome mystery of the universe eludes us not because we are innately inferior, but because our language continually robs us."

"How so?" Sheeb implored, straining to understand.

"You and I are having this conversation in a language that was created through a synthesis of European-based languages. The very nature of this language is to create and sustain the illusion that there is a subject and an object. The basic grammar of our language requires this dichotomy. But," Ran said excitedly, "this is an illusion of the most insidious kind. There is no you and me. There is only one being, one vast interconnected experience of the universe. You and I are merely fragments in this vast mosaic. That's what I realized when I sent the cube out of this dimension into another. Not only this, but because I was operating from the intrinsic error in our language, I had no idea that I was violating a fundamental and universal law."

"Which is?" Sheeb asked.

"That we are interconnected to all things and all times, and we are not to interfere or contaminate other dimensions of consciousness."

"There's another odd thing about this."

Ran started laughing. "The whole thing's odd, Sheeb, odder than we could ever imagine."

"Vollen said that just before you 'translated' the cube, several people in the lab heard a low insect-like sound, and some saw a purplish light around the cube. But neither the video cameras nor the recording equipment picked up any of it. What was going on?"

"Hyperspace," Ran offered.

Sheeb motioned Ran to continue.

"The physical reality that you and I experience with our senses is the result of subtler forces operating at the atomic and subatomic levels."

"Yes, I understand that," Sheeb said with slight exasperation.

"There are subtler levels than the subatomic, but our science has not yet made contact with them because they are subtler than any instrument is capable of detecting. One of these is the level of pure consciousness, or hyperspace. It is through hyperspace that consciousness coalesces into sub-atomic particles and forces."

"Okay, so you've got a kind of Unified Theory of Consciousness and Matter here, but what does that have to do with insect sounds and purple light?"

"Everything," Ran said. "The sound of consciousness coalescing into matter is like the sound made by billions of crickets or cicadas. But it is not a sound you hear with your ears. It's a sound you hear with your mind. If your mind is quiet enough and attuned properly, you can hear it, though no one else around you would."

"And the light?" Sheeb asked, genuinely intrigued by Ran's esoteric babble.

"The purple light is actually a kind of liquid that links this world with that of hyperspace. Certain shamanic rituals from indigenous peoples use this light to enter into a timeless dimension, the precursor, if you will, of matter and our physical universe." Ran paused for a moment and took a deep breath. "The nature of this hyperspatial liquid is of a unique substance. It is essentially densely packed language."

"Language?"

"Yes, Sheeb. Language...it's a kind of intricate mosaic comprised of infinite levels of meaning."

Ran and Sheeb's conversation was interrupted by Centauri. The dog had turned toward the door and was growling. Moments later Hoffman appeared at the glass door carrying his black medical bag. Sheeb walked over to the door and slid it open.

"Good morning, Dr. Sheeb."

"Dr. Hoffman..." Sheeb motioned him in. "Aren't you a little early for Dr. Farr's injection?"

"Well yes, but—uh... I have a lot of work in the lab this morning and I thought I'd get this over with."

"OK, I'll be outside." Sheeb stepped through the door and called Centauri. Walking over to the railing, Sheeb looked out across the water to where the meteor had disappeared hours earlier. The muted grays and pinks of early dawn had pasteled themselves across the sky and the sun was just slipping above the horizon. Perhaps Ran was right. Where was Vollen?

Centauri brushed up against Sheeb's leg, trying to soothe his master's concern. Sheeb reached down and stroked his side. The air exploded with the sound of a helicopter as it swooped down over the trees to the main building. Sheeb looked up and caught the glimmer of a man's sunglasses as the craft rocketed toward the mansion.

Looking down, Buchner watched a man and a dog peering up at him. "So that's Alan Sheeb."

A muscular man in his late twenties leaned over and looked out the window. A smirk crossed his face as he pulled himself back in. "Not for long, Mr. Buchner, not for long."

CHAPTER TWENTY-EIGHT

Charles Buchner sat in the dim light of Darkos's office, the gold light of early morning flooding the room through the east window.

Torn stood in the corner of the room, fascinated with the giant lizard. Buchner looked at his assistant for a moment, admiring the thick muscles of his back. Sensing someone's eyes on him, Torn turned, looked at Buchner, and then turned back to the lizard. Buchner admired Torn's cruel and haunting beauty, but it wasn't his Adonis-like bearing that pleased Buchner the most. Neither was it his extraordinary strength that had enabled him to beat everyone in his training pod, including his instructors. These qualities were pleasing enough, but it was the precision with which Torn killed that could take Buchner's breath away. Buchner had seen him break the necks of his victims with such elegance, such gentle harsh-ness that they seemed to surrender and melt into their demise. Torn was an artist, and his palette the many faces of death. He had more ways to kill a woman, a man or child than Buchner had ever known existed. And all that power, elegance and artistry belonged to him. Torn was absolutely and totally dedicated. He would, without a moment's hesitation, give up his young life for his employer, should he ask for it. The brain implants insured it. And if the day came when Torn would have to kill himself to protect Buchner, he knew that Torn would take his own life with the same elegance and precision with which he killed his victims.

Precision was something Buchner demanded, from the cut of his Italian suits to the German ballbearing Reichstalt in his right hand. The platinum and titanium pen was legendary among the affluent and the elite, but that wasn't why Buchner owned one. He admired it for the precision with which the ink chamber slid up and down through the alloy cylinder. Sixty-four titanium ball bearings rolled forward in the ink chamber and its elegant sloping point at the slightest pressure. Buchner liked the feel of it, and had developed the comforting habit of engaging the pen's chamber whenever he was nervous or irritated.

Torn had long ago recognized the Reichstalt ritual, and knew enough to become wary whenever Buchner pulled the pen from his vest pocket. He turned now, at the familiar sound of the pen, to see him looking at the gray carpet. Perhaps he was thinking of what lay ahead. Who knew? Buchner revealed so little of himself to anyone. Torn heard someone approaching.

The door opened and Darkos stepped into the room. Reaching for the light switch, she was stopped by Buchner's husky voice.

"No overhead lights, please." Buchner's hand waved the air.

"As you wish." Darkos crossed the room to her desk and nodded at Torn standing by the terrarium. Darkos slipped into her overstuffed chair and pulled herself up to the desk. "So you got here sooner than you thought."

"Obviously." Buchner said.

Darkos cleared her throat and cursed under her breath, reminding herself that Buchner did not go in for small talk. Darkos pulled a manila folder from her desk and handed it to him. "These are my observations and suggestions on Dr. Farr."

Buchner opened the envelope and slid the small computer disk into his hand. "I appreciate your thoroughness, Ellen. Now how about briefing me so I don't have to spend my valuable time in front of a terminal."

"Certainly." Darkos reached for a paper clip on her desk and fingered it as she spoke. "Dr. Farr has been diagnosed as suffering from psychotic shock. As of this moment, Alan Sheeb has been unable to get any information from him regarding the Mind War Machine, and it is unlikely he will ever be able to do so."

Buchner pressed the Reichstalt in his right hand, the tension in his hand translating into the smooth rotation of titanium ball bearings. Torn shifted his weight uncomfortably. "Why is Alan Sheeb still alive? I believe I suggested that you terminate him."

The room suddenly brightened as sunlight poured through the venetian blinds. Darkos raised a hand to her eyes. The blinds had cut the sun into ribbons of golden light now streaming into Darkos's office. Squinting to see Buchner's face made Darkos uneasy.

"Torn," she asked, "would you close those blinds?"

The terminator silently crossed the room and closed the venetians. The room passed into a soft darkness. Darkos flipped on her desk lamp.

"You were saying?" she asked.

"I was saying I don't understand why you haven't killed Alan Sheeb yet." Buchner replied, obviously irritated.

Darkos watched Torn as he walked back to the sleeping reptile in the corner of the room. "He's not important now."

"I don't understand."

"Dr. Hoffman injected a memory suppressant into Dr. Farr, and there is no way Alan Sheeb will ever get the information he is looking for. When we are ready to Deep Mind Probe, I will simply have Hoffman administer an antidote."

"What if Alan Sheeb got the information about the Mind War Machine before you gave him this..."

"Memerol 57," Darkos offered. "I don't see how that would be possible. He hasn't been here that long and I have had Farr carefully monitored."

"Where is he now?" Buchner asked.

"At the guest cottage."

"With Sheeb?" he asked.

"Yes."

"Allowing them to be alone is hardly careful monitoring."

"I had no choice. Vollen went above me."

"Oh, yes, Vollen." Buchner leaned back in his chair. "And where is he now? Have you thought about how you will deal with him?"

"He's dead." Darkos noticed Torn becoming visibly more interested in the conversation.

"How?" Buchner asked.

"I caught him stealing one of the land transports. He was probably planning an escape."

"So you just shot him?" Buchner asked incredulously.

"Yes, he pissed me off."

Torn laughed out loud and leaned against the terrarium. His laughter stopped abruptly and he looked at the giant lizard as he spoke to Darkos. "What was it like?" His voice seemed far away, half in trance. He turned and looked at Darkos.

"It was marvelous," Darkos replied. "His body flashed like oil set on fire and then he exploded into a tornado of burning gas."

"And the sound?" Torn's eyes slightly dilated.

"Incredible."

Torn grinned.

"You've seen a vaporization before?" Darkos asked.

"A few." By the sound of his words and the look in his eyes, Darkos knew that he enjoyed them as much as she did.

Buchner broke in on their discussion. "You two can discuss the aesthetics of termination later."

"Yes, sir." Torn snapped to attention.

"I assume the Deep Mind Probe is prepared and ready?"

"Yes, sir."

CHAPTER TWENTY-NINE

Hoffman smiled and raised the syringe into the air, a single droplet of the clear liquid shimmering at the very tip of the stainless steel point. Ran barely noticed. He had witnessed this so many times before, the patterns in the linoleum tile were much more interesting.

Ran felt himself merging with the yellows and blues that swirled around each other across the floor. He swayed to a beautiful music, a music that no one else even knew existed. The lush strings of the blues were enfolding the strident trumpets of the yellows. For a moment he smelled daisies. He hardly noticed the prick in his right arm as Hoffman injected the Memerol. As Ran followed the patterns of color into the center of the floor, the music rose into one last crescendo and a single tear shimmered in Ran's eye.

Grabbing his black bag, Hoffman took one last look at Ran, slumped over, staring with rapture at the nondescript floor. The director of Biological Resources left the room.

Ran heard the sliding glass door in the kitchen open and then close. Something was wrong. He could feel it in the energy patterns that swirled about his body. Usually they rotated in long slow arcs around him, but now they eddied in torrents. His head began to swim as the Memerol found its way into his brain. Ran tried to steady himself. The muscles in his gut spasmed and the room suddenly turned cold. His teeth chattered uncontrollably. Clothes, that's what he needed. Steadying himself, Ran rose from the chair. His hands went limp. Gravity pulled at him as if trying to drag him through the floor. Staggering into the hallway, Ran bumped against the wall and collapsed.

Memerol had been designed for persons in normal to anxious states of consciousness. It had never been intended for someone blissed out on endorphins. Later research would verify what would be called Endorphin Reversal (ER), a highly toxic state. Even now the Memerol was shredding electrons from the outer shells of neurotransmitters. What had been meant to suppress memory was now obliterating it. The cold reached into Ran's core. Dragging himself across the floor, he headed for Sheeb's bedroom, where a sweat suit lay next to the bed. His shaking hands pulled the UC Berkeley sweatshirt toward him, but his fingers went limp. The Memerol had entered the motor cortex of the brain, and denied its crop of messengers, his nervous system had simply forgotten how to move Ran's muscles.

The lethal chemical was spreading like a deadly sea throughout the cortex. Images from the past flitted through Ran's mind like moths before their mass extinction. Centauri seemed restless. He kept sniffing and scratching the glass door. Sheeb let him in, and then followed the dog into the kitchen. Centauri ran down the hall ahead of him.

The sudden image of Ran stretched out on the floor flashed through Sheeb's mind. Centauri was calling him. Sheeb careened down the hall and into his bedroom. Ran lay on the floor beside the bed, his outstretched arm not quite reaching Sheeb's sweatshirt. His body was shaking and he seemed to be in shock. Ripping the covers off the bed, Sheeb pulled Ran's feet up onto the mattress and tucked the quilt around his naked body.

Sitting beside his friend, Sheeb placed a hand at the back of Ran's head and dropped into sync. Ran's brain was panicked. Massive armies of white blood cells were swarming through the bloodstream, searching for the toxic attacker. But Memerol had been created by man, not nature, and millions of years of evolution were left impotent by the strange invader.

The chemical had just found its way into the hippocampus. The ancient part of the brain, shocked by the onslaught of chemical madness, was forgetting how to remember. Fragments of memories from the past floated into consciousness in some great neural flotsam. Each experience encoded within the brain was unraveling itself. Sheeb sat in abject horror as he watched the mind of his friend dissolve into nothingness.

The smell of perfume and a soft nipple against his mouth...Ran's memories as a baby passed through Sheeb's mind. The loving touch of his mother's hand against his skin... and then...the crack of a baseball bat and the hardball arcing its way into the air, the sweet smell of summer everywhere. Everything Ran ever experienced poured through Sheeb's awestruck mind. Ran's first love...the fragrant moistness of her sex....his moments of loneliness...the torture of adolescence. Everything, every thought, every feeling passed through Sheeb. And in that moment of unraveling, Ran's great love for Sheeb...the great immensity of it passed through Sheeb's mind.

Sheeb's throat tried to choke back the tears but they poured through him anyway. The room filled with the sound of his weeping. Drying his eyes as best he could, Sheeb tried to keep track of Ran as the Memerol moved into the deeper structures of the brain. The last of Ran's memories ejaculated into oblivion as the chemical assassin moved deeper into the limbic core, home of ancestral memories and the regulation of breathing.

It all happened in a moment. The respiratory center forgot how to breathe. The lungs fell silent as galaxies of cells panicked. Without oxygen the remaining neurons inside the brain fell into a carbon dioxide death. Trillions of stars within Ran's body went dim and the brilliant light of Ran's mind turned dark as his world disappeared.

CHAPTER THIRTY

Sheeb gently stroked Ran's head. Outside, beyond the large window that overlooked the sea, the rising sun was pouring molten gold into the room and across Ran's chest.

Sheeb had that anti-gravity feeling again, as if everything in the room was floating. Centauri rose from the carpet where he had been sitting and padded his way over to Sheeb, pushing his nose under Sheeb's outstretched arm.

The sound of a Land Transport filled the air as it pulled up in front of the cottage. Moments later, the glass door to the kitchen slid open. Centauri dropped close to the floor and growled. Sheeb got up and walked into the hallway, Centauri following close behind.

Sheeb stepped into the living room and stood by the couch as Darkos and two men entered the room. Darkos saw Sheeb and held out her hand toward her companions. "Dr. Sheeb, I'd like you to meet Charles Buchner, my associate on this project, and his assistant." Sheeb nodded. Centauri started to growl. Sheeb told him, tele-pathically, to be silent.

"Where's Dr. Farr?" Darkos asked.

"He's dead." Sheeb motioned toward the back room.

"I don't believe it." Darkos crossed the room into the hallway and walked toward the bedroom.

Buchner waved her silent. "How did this happen?" His voice sounded strained.

Sheeb, Buchner, and Torn followed Darkos into the bedroom where Ran lay sprawled out on the floor. Darkos turned noticeably uncomfortable. Her jaws were clenched and the coloration of her skin paled. Sheeb continued. "Everything's gone now. Whatever memories he may have had have been totally erased."

"But how did this happen?" Buchner asked, obviously angered.

"I suggest you check with Hoffman. Ran was fine until after his injection. Whatever Hoffman injected into Ran reacted with his blood chemistry. Ran died of suffocation."

Buchner's right hand blurred as it slapped Darkos in the face. The room filled with the sound of flesh smacking flesh. "You fucking incompetent bitch!" Darkos backed off like an animal that had just been brutalized by her master.

Centauri dropped low to the floor and growled again. Without missing a beat, Buchner pointed to the animal even as he looked at Darkos recovering from the shock of his attack.

"I want that dog out of here. See if you can do that right!"

"Wait a minute," pleaded Sheeb. "What is this all about?"

Buchner looked at him for a moment and raised a hand into the air. "This!" He snapped his fingers, and Torn pulled out a laser, directing it at Sheeb. Sheeb looked into his blue-green eyes for a moment, their luster reminding him of summer skies off Morocco. Strange how the brain connected things that weren't truly connected, and odder still were those times when the mind made its peculiar logic.

The leader of the mind thieves motioned everyone back into the living room and a waiting valise. "I imagine you recognize this." Buchner placed the attaché case on a desk and opened it to reveal the gleaming aluminum body of a Deep Mind Probe.

Sheeb nodded. It was clear that Buchner intended to rip apart Sheeb's memory in search of anything he may have discovered about the Mind War Machine. Oblivion hovered just minutes away.

Sheeb needed information about the intruders, and fast. His only hope was to drop into sync past the storm of adrenaline raging in his bloodstream. All he really wanted to do was throw all of them against the wall and break their necks. But that would have to wait. Calling on every resource he had, Sheeb finally managed to adjust his own brain waves and drop into the calm of deep alpha. He scanned the room and the three people surrounding him. From the calm of alpha, it seemed as if they were all underwater.

Darkos was still in shock, badly shaken. Her only solace was a fantasy about firing Hoffman and the terror that would bring.

Most of Torn's attention was on Sheeb, the laser poised elegantly in his left hand. A small portion of awareness was focused on Charles Buchner, who needed only to utter one word for Torn to vaporize Sheeb into bloody steam on the spot.

Sheeb watched Buchner setting up the Deep Mind Probe. The intruder's emotions were seething like hydrogen gas threatening to explode at any moment. Sheeb caught a random thought passing through the Buchner's mind— a command to vaporize Centauri.

Sheeb immediately directed his attention to the dog, and sensing the familiar net of energy around his brain, the animal looked up. "Do as they say, Centauri. Follow her outside."

Buchner turned and looked at Sheeb with an odd expression, and then turned back to the Mind Probe. As Centauri padded his way over to Darkos, Sheeb telepathically directed the dog to act submissive and to go out onto the deck by the open window and sit where he couldn't be seen. As the dog stepped up to Darkos, he lowered his head and looked to the floor. Darkos was pleased to regain some respect, even if it was coming from an animal.

Grabbing him by the collar, she led him out the door, into the living room, through the kitchen, and out onto the deck. The glass door slid shut behind her, and Darkos paused in the kitchen to get a drink of water.

"Place your laser on stun." Buchner glanced at Torn as he unwrapped the metal leads for the Mind Probe. "If he so much as moves, shoot him."

"Yes, Sir." Torn's eyes narrowed slightly as he looked at Sheeb's stomach. He lowered the device just enough so that any blast of photons would lash into Sheeb's gut.

Sheeb had experienced the stun of a laser during a weapons training accident years ago. It was not a pleasant experience. When set on stun, the searing heat was not enough to kill or vaporize, but it did burn and with a pain unimaginable, driving itself deeper and deeper into the tissue until one went delirious with pain. Torn was obviously pleased at the prospect of hurling the burning into Sheeb's umbilicus.

The light through the open window caught one of the brass leads in Buchner's hand and the room filled with a flash of gold. Buchner walked over to Sheeb. "Take off your shirt."

Sheeb obliged and pulled the cotton sweatshirt off, letting it drop to the floor. Buchner stuck one of the electrodes into the crevice of his ribs, just under the meaty part of his pectoral. The harsh coolness of metal caught Sheeb's attention for a moment. As Buchner pulled the second contact from its adhesive backing, Sheeb saw Darkos walking into the living room from the kitchen. Time was running out. With just six more contacts on his chest and head, the Mind Probe would be operational.

Sheeb reached out to Centauri, the telepathic web of their bonding passing through the walls, unknown to the intruders. As Sheeb drew an imaginary line in his mind through the open window and into Torn's left hand, Buchner pressed the second contact under Sheeb's left collar bone. Reaching back toward the Mind Probe, he grabbed the next contact from the attaché case and pulled it from its backing.

In his mind, Sheeb screamed "NOW!" Centauri leapt through the window, the air suddenly blurred by his massive body and shattered glass. Torn screamed as the animal ripped into his left hand. The laser fell to the floor as sharp canines tore an artery loose from the flesh of his hand. Blood spurted into the air.

Sheeb bellowed and kicked Buchner in the crotch. The man dropped to the floor. Sheeb lunged for the laser, picked it up, and fired at Darkos as she ran toward him. The pulse of photons screamed into her right shoulder, and she moaned as the polyester in her blouse melted, the heat singeing her and driving itself deeper into her body. She fell unconscious against the door.

Torn managed to shake Centauri

from his arm, and cursing, he kicked him in the chest and threw the animal against the wall. Enraged, Sheeb turned on his side and fired the laser into Torn's gut.

Stunned, Torn fell against the wall and looked at Sheeb as the air filled with smoke from his melting shirt. His eyes rolled back into his head and he fell against the wall. Torn slid to the floor moaning with pain. His left hand fell loose by his side, and a river of dark red blood pulsed onto the carpet.

Turning to Buchner, Sheeb motioned him to stand up. The would-be mind thief backed up against the opposite wall. Sheeb walked over to see that Centauri was okay, a little shaken was all. The animal had had the air knocked out of him, but he was all right. Sheeb pulled a kerchief from his trousers and tossed it to Buchner. "Here, make a tourniquet for his arm unless you want him to die for his carelessness."

Buchner stopped the flow of Torn's blood and looked up at Sheeb. The pulse of light from Sheeb's laser sliced into Buchner's shoulder and he fell unconscious against the wall.

Sheeb moved the control switch on the laser from stun to vaporize, and blasted the Mind Probe. The screeching sound of vaporizing aluminum filled the room as clouds of ionized metal swirled up to the ceiling.

Sheeb quickly walked to the bedroom where Ran was still lying on the floor and stooped down, pulling him up into his arms. For a moment, as Sheeb regained his balance, Ran's hand fell to the floor. Sheeb struggled to his feet, and carried the body outside to the Land Transport. Gently touching Ran's chest, Sheeb slid his body into the cargo area, and then closed the door.

As he entered the LT, Sheeb motioned Centauri in beside him. The electric motors hummed as he pulled the van around and headed for the main gate. Passing into a dark archway of ferns, the air suddenly turned moist and cool. Centauri pushed his head out from one of the windows to drink in the rich smells of humus.

The LT pulled out from the dark fern-like womb into the large field of giant Venus's fly-traps. The strange botanicals seemed oddly luminescent as the van rolled through banks of fog, the morning blanket of dew having been transformed into clouds of steam. Droplets of water hung quivering from the upturned mouths of the carnivorous plants. Everywhere, Sheeb could smell the exotic odor of death. In the middle of the deathly garden a lone moth stumbled into the portal of one of the large predators. The plant snapped shut, and the soft iridescent body was swallowed into the botanical's dark cavern. Only the insect's wings remained outside, beating helplessly against the tightening grip of its captor.

The road suddenly curved out of the field and onto the main driveway. Up ahead, Sheeb could see the gate and its waiting guard. As he pulled up to the checkpoint, Sheeb moved the controls on the laser from vaporize to stun. The guard stepped up to the van for the LT's clearance papers and then fell onto the asphalt drive unconscious from the force of the photon stream.

Getting out of the LT, Sheeb walked into the guard house and opened the main gate. Stepping out onto the pavement again, Sheeb slipped the laser back from stun to vaporize and leaned into the small enclosure. The communications computer and telephone burst into flame as the laser sliced into them, the screeching sound of vaporizing aluminum again ripping the air. When the guard came to, it would take him a half-hour to walk back to the Bosk mansion for help.

Sheeb hopped back into the van and pulled out onto the highway. There, in the disc player, was Jeff's copy of the Vulvonics. For the hell of it, Sheeb flipped it on. The air quivered with the pelvic pulse of the Vulvonics' second hit, "Out of Here."

CHAPTER THIRTY-ONE

Alpha Lyra was still sitting in the morning shadow of Hangar B where Vollen had left it. Walking up to the shuttle, Sheeb inspected the craft's aluminum skin and landing gear, everything seemingly in order. Pausing by the entry hatch, Sheeb spoke to the onboard computer through the communications port, a small recessed panel barely noticeable through the shuttle's insignia.

"Alan Sheeb, requesting entry."

There was a moment of silence as the computer analyzed Sheeb's voice pattern against the one stored in its memory. The light on the panel shifted green and the side slid away to reveal the hand scan, a second identification security check.

Sheeb pressed his right hand against the Plexiglas shield. An orange-tinted light cascaded up and around his fingers as the computer fathomed the micron-high mountains and valleys of flesh that made up Alan Sheeb's hand.

"You may enter." The computer's electronic voice reverberated off the side wall of the hangar. Sheeb hastily glanced around. They were still alone. He walked back and slid open the side doors to the transport. Centauri bounded onto the concrete parking area. Sheeb reached in and pulled Ran's naked body into his arms. The thirty-second walk to the shuttle seemed endless. A soft burning was at the back of Sheeb's throat and he pulled his head back to avert tears. Glancing upward, he watched a large cumulous cloud crawling its way across the sky like a giant turtle.

Centauri approached the door of the shuttle and barked. Sheeb told him to enter and then followed the dog into the orbiter. He reached over with an elbow and punched the control panel for the door. Hidden motors hummed as the metal hatch slid shut.

Placing Ran gently on the floor, Sheeb stepped out of the holding area and walked over to his seat and the control panel. With the flip of a toggle switch, the air crackled as an invisible wall of electromagnetism enclosed the holding area and Ran's body.

Walking to one of the lockers, Sheeb stripped off his clothes, toweled the sweat off his body, and slipped into a nylon jumpsuit. Centauri was already sitting in the co-pilot's chair. Taking a seat beside the canine, Sheeb turned on the pre-takeoff circuits. As he punched in the co-ordinates for Bethesda, the onboard computer checked the engines and fuel lines as well as all secondary systems. Ironically, it would take less time for Alpha Lyra to reach Bethesda by rocketing westward into low Earth orbit than it would to simply cross the continent on the jet stream. The computer signaled all circuits ready, and Sheeb reached over to the recessed switches for the power boosters.

The small shuttle rolled out onto the short runway, and the air filled with the sound of 500,000 pounds of thrust. Rising from the Earth, the orbiter shook from the combined surge of four Rockwells. Mercilessly, the harsh fingers of gravity shoved him back into his seat. The white sands of the California desert blurred beneath them as the Sierra mountain range faded behind in the distance like a dark border of paper maché.

Arcing upward, the shuttle streaked toward the stars. Monitoring the computer closely, Sheeb reached for the manual override. He did not care to repeat what had happened earlier. There was no need for alarm. On cue, the onboard microprocessor turned off the power boosters and leveled the nose off at 50 miles above the Pacific Ocean. A clipboard floated in the air near where it had shaken loose on takeoff. Alpha Lyra had just entered zero gravity.

Checking Centauri's straps, Sheeb noticed Ran floating serenely behind the invisible walls of the holding area. He seemed to be floating in water, the illusion created by the soft blue-green light of the luminescent panel.

Leaning back in his seat, Sheeb reached over and activated the Orbital Release switch. The holding area crackled as it prepared to dump its cargo into the vacuum of space. Sheeb's mind raced back through holomemories of his university days with Ran. One night, plastered on tequila and ouzo, Ran had staggered from table to table in the rathskellar announcing that he wanted his body to be sent into space when he died. Little did he know that on an autumn day some twelve years later he would have his wish over the island of Guam. Hidden panels above the holding area slid open and Ran's naked body floated out into space. Beneath him, the Earth rolled its way around the sun, unaware of the new satellite. Far beneath Ran's body, now floating in orbit, a young Guamanian snorkeled for pearls in the autumn light.

Sheeb sighed and took a deep breath as the holding area's doors slid shut. Leaning back in his seat, Sheeb closed his eyes for a moment. It lasted only an instant, but the impression was vivid. A green cloud passed soundlessly through Sheeb's mind, and from within the cloud, it felt as if he had once again entered Ran's mind.

"My god, that's it!" Sheeb yelled. Centauri barked at the sudden break in the silence.

"It's okay, Centauri, it's okay." Sheeb rubbed the dog's head reassuringly.

The animal looked into Sheeb's eyes for a moment and then returned its gaze to the blue orb of the earth beneath them.

Of course! When Ran had died, Sheeb had been in sync with him, tracking him to the edge of oblivion. As Ran's mind unspiraled itself, the tracings went into Sheeb's own brain. Everything Ran had ever experienced was now spread out along the fingertips of Sheeb's own neural pathways.

"Everything..." Sheeb whispered the word into the silence of the cabin. Somewhere in Sheeb's own mind, somewhere within this floating green cloud, the riddle of the Mind War Machine was waiting to be revealed. Sheeb checked the telemetry and all support systems of the shuttle—everything in order. It would be safe to drop into the deep state of theta and explore the cloud.

Like a scuba diver searching for treasure, Sheeb sank deeper and deeper into the murky fog. He felt it first, before he saw it—a small frog, its cool, soft belly... and the small fingers of a six-year-old boy sliding across the amphibian's abdomen, the smell of moist foliage filling the air. The image changed, and Sheeb felt a blast of cold air, heard the sound of skis sliding down crisp snow as the towering peak of the Matterhorn rose through low-hung clouds. Off in the distance, the sky turned dark with cloud as the smell and promise of new snow drifted into the valley. Knees bent and thighs flexed as Ran turned into one of the side paths, following a young sweetheart.

And then a memory of Sheeb. He and Ran were standing on a pier at sunset as Earth's great star set into the Pacific Ocean. Ran looked at Sheeb for a moment, and in the reddish hue of the setting sun reached over and put his arm around his friend.

Tears filled his eyes, as Sheeb remembered the event both from his own memory and from the memory of his lost companion. How odd and how bitter-sweet to hold two minds within one.

A strange buzzing sound passed through the cloud, and Sheeb noticed the carbonite cube hovering in the murkiness. A haunting opalescence pulsed from the sides of the object, and he felt himself being pulled sideways, as if something were trying to keep him from looking any closer. But years of "tracking" other minds through the aftermath of Deep Mind Probes paid off as Sheeb rotated his own angle of perception to match the rotation of the strange cube.

The image stabilized, and a thin slit of light cut through the darkness as the cube began to unfold itself. In the instant of its opening, Sheeb understood the Mind War Machine. The entirety of it lay spread out before him.

Sheeb could feel Ran back in the lab. The carbonite cube lay in front of him. Metal leads ran from his head to a microprocessor. His brain ached from hours of solid concentration. A single thought form held in the arms of Ran's own mind floated in the magnetic psi-bank of the computer complex. The psi-bank tracked all neural activity and recorded all impressions that entered Ran's opened mind. It then created a resonant frequency that matched the activity occurring within his brain. By oscillating this frequency with the electromagnetic frequency of his own brain, he increased the power of his intention ten-fold.

There was the ripping sound of something being torn open, and a sudden wave of energy rushed through Ran's mind and into the computers. A strange sound filled the room, like the sound of thousands upon thousands of crickets singing. Ran looked at the cube. Something was floating around it. A purple liquid light was swirling around the carbonite, and in the eddies, there were stars.

Ran's eyes blurred as he realized all things are expressions of one fundamental consciousness. In that single moment of clarity all the myriad forms in the universe, including the universe itself, appeared as a mirage, a ghost image without substance. Ran's brain reeled from the enormity of his realization.

There was the sensation of something burning inside his mind, and then suddenly he was inexplicably aware of everything within a one-mile radius... aware of the atoms spinning in the walls of the laboratory... the thoughts and desires of his assistants...the geese outside on Weirman Lake...the smell of seabreeze...and the clouds drifting eastward. The river of images and feelings avalanched through Ran's quivering mind. An explosion of light seared him, the room seeming to collapse around him. There were shouts.

"It's gone! The cube is gone!"

But Ran had been wrong. In his strain to translate the cube, he was not able to follow it after its departure from this dimension. Ran had assumed that it was now in another physical dimension, but something far more dazzling had occurred. At the moment of translation, the atomic forces that had bound the carbonite together were suspended. The stability of the cube gave way to a riot of subatomic particles, each one following its own anarchistic inclinations. In that instant, a microscopic black hole, the size of one carbon atom, formed at the center of the quickly disintegrating cube.

The minuscule black hole began to devour every shred of matter that had been the cube, swallowing the carbonite in less time than the high-speed video cameras were capable of recording. Within a nanosecond, the densely compressed matter exploded in the heated inferno of the black hole, spewing pure energy and gas into a parallel universe. A new star was born in the blackness of space.

CHAPTER THIRTY-ONE

Ran had no way of knowing
this, but five billion years later, there would be planets encircling the new sun. In another four hundred million years, life
would appear. The future inhabitants of the planet would
eventually develop complex language, poetry, and science.
Their greatest pastime would be cosmology. Theories as to
their origins abounded, each one attempting an explanation
for why their world showed so many traces of carbon while
the element could scarcely be found anywhere else in their
universe. Their greatest minds would wrestle with the enigma, never suspecting that their very existence was the result
of a laboratory experiment gone awry in a world and a universe they would never see.

Such is the paradox and irony
of a universe so closely woven together.

Sheeb left his inner world, and
swimming up from the deep calm of theta, he opened his eyes.
The shuttle had altered its orbit and was now hurtling through
space high above the waste lands of Mongolia. The onboard
computer signaled another alteration of course and fired the
small orbiting rockets on either side of the craft. Alpha Lyra
arched onto her side and slid down the globe toward the
Himalayas of northern India.

It must have been the after-
effect of experiencing Ran's mind. But there was a sudden feeling of opening between Sheeb's eyes, and a sensation of swirling
light in the center of his head. The Earth, far below, seemed suddenly possessed by a light and a power he had never experienced. Everywhere Sheeb looked, the entire planet seethed with a
tempest of feeling he had never imagined. How was it possible?
How could it be? Had he gone mad?

He felt beggars dying in
Calcutta, their wasted bodies carried away by street cleaners in
the early morning light...and then the sweet smell of baked
bread and coffee wafted in the air of a street in Paris...a feeble

old man in Manhattan sitting on a park bench watched two young lovers crossing the street hand in hand...pigeons flew upward to a gray sky over Chicago as commuters crawled their way by the Great Lake. In Los Angeles, on Venice Beach, a fifteen year old runaway huddled up against a dumpster as roller skaters rolled passed him unaware...and far out in the Pacific an ancient humpback whale died...its massive body slowly drifting toward the sea floor.

The images kept rushing through Sheeb's outstretched mind, the visions burning him, his brain reeling from the enormity of such life. His head throbbed. "Too much," he moaned, "too much." As if heeding his command, the strange perceptions stopped and the swirling lights inside his head subsided.

CHAPTER THIRTY-TWO

The re-entry alert screeched through the cabin as Alpha Lyra arced itself into the Earth's atmosphere above the west coast of Africa. Sheeb reached over to the computer, checking his telemetry—nothing unusual. A thin carpet of white cirrus clouds lay stretched out from the mouth of the Mediterranean all the way down to the Ivory Coast.

In minutes, the vast continent of Africa gave way to the rolling waves of the Atlantic Ocean, and making her final approach, Alpha Lyra soared over the eastern arm of Virginia into Maryland. Ninety minutes after take-off, Sheeb set the small craft onto the runway at the shuttle port near Bethesda. A cab took him to the offices of BioTechnologies while Centauri remained behind with the shuttle. Sheeb would pick him up after his conference with Bach. The dog could be left on his own for hours at a time without any seeming discomfort. Valkovian Labradors were known for their ability to entertain themselves, a quality Sheeb found most admirable.

Sheeb hailed a cab at the port, and on the way to Bach's office he wondered what shape he'd find him in. Had the financier fought off the starkiller, or had the "hell hole of gravity" swallowed him?

The lab technician held out his hand. "Hi, I'm Marc."

"Alan Sheeb."

"Yes, we've been expecting you. Mr. Bach asked me to show you in as soon as you arrived."

With an air of assurance, the young man led Sheeb toward Bach's office. Pausing by the door, Marc turned to Sheeb. "There is something I should tell you."

"Yes?"

"We had to do major surgery to save him...or perhaps," the technician looked up to one of the corners of the room, "it depends on what part of him you're talking about."

"What are you talking about?" Sheeb asked.

"Alfred Bach is floating in a tank inside this room." The uneasy technician took a breath and then swallowed. "Not all of him that is, just his brain."

"His brain?" Sheeb asked.

"It was the only way to save him. By isolating the brain, we hoped that we could stop the deterioration of the brain stem."

"And?" There was challenge in Sheeb's voice.

The young man looked to the floor as if the right words might be found lurking somewhere in the carpet. For a moment, he just stood there looking down and shaking his head. "We can't stop it." He looked up at Sheeb. "There's nothing we can do."

"I see." Sheeb reached for the door and pushed it open. Stepping into the vastness of Bach's office, Sheeb could see a Plexiglas cube bathed in golden light at the other end of the massive room. The hundreds of artifacts were dimly lit and gave the impression, as they shaped a path toward the gleaming glass and metal of the cube, that Sheeb had stepped into an ancient and forbidden temple.

Marc's voice turned suddenly soft, as if he too had been overcome by the unusual sanctity of the room. "I'll leave you alone. If you need me, just call."

Sheeb nodded, the door closing behind him. As he passed his way through the sea of relics toward the gleaming cube, Sheeb noticed a suit of armor to his right, and suddenly he had the oddest feeling—as if he had been catapulted back to medieval Europe. Bathed in golden light, Bach's brain was resting in the lower half of its skull. The top half of the cranium had been removed and the visual effect was as if the brain was resting inside a cup. The sight of Bach's brain woven with the strange feeling of being in Medieval Europe was transformed within Sheeb's mind into an image of the Holy Grail. The Grail was the cup used by Jesus during the Last Supper and reenacted in the ritual of Holy Communion by his followers ever since. Scenes of knights and pilgrims, monks and whores filled Sheeb's mind as thoughts of the Great Crusades washed through him. Strange how the image of the Grail had spewed Europe into one of its most maddening and irrational odysseys. And stranger still was the enigma of the Grail itself. The Knights Templar never found the Grail, and if the poets are right it was because they were looking in the wrong place—for the Holy Grail was not to be found outside oneself, but inside.

He had never thought about it before, but Sheeb agreed that the mythology of the Grail could easily be transferred onto the human brain. And why not? The Grail was believed by medieval pilgrims to impart magical powers to those who had the good fortune of finding it. And while the messianic cup was never actually found, the brain, progenitor to all of man's creations sat silently resting within the Holy Grail of every human. It was through the powers of the brain and mind that the greatest achievements and the most terrible horrors of man had been achieved. It sat hidden, bound by darkness within its bony skull, rarely seen and thus all the more taken for granted.

Sheeb shook off the feeling as he stepped up to the cube. There, floating serenely in yellow-gold light, Bach's brain lay revealed, the ridges of the neocortex reminding Sheeb, oddly, of walnuts.

Lowering himself to the floor like an acolyte, Sheeb knelt in front of the luminescent device. The room was silent but for the soft hum of motors feeding oxygen to the suspension cube holding Bach's brain. A lone power cord stretched like a serpent over the burgundy carpet to an outlet on the wall.

Sheeb closed his eyes and dropped into sync, the deep calm of alpha overtaking him as he approached Bach's mind. The deeper structures of Bach's brain had already died. Only the neocortex, folding over itself with a lifetime of memories, remained. Without the hemoliquid circulating through the suspension cube, this last vestige of Bach would perish within minutes.

Drifting past the physical structure of Bach's brain into his mind felt like swimming into dark and turbulent waters. Images flowed into Sheeb's mind from out of Bach's own sea of holodreams. The resplendent figure of a woman cast in marble somersaulted through the air, her body and gown of stone but her eyes alive. And catching a glimpse of them, Sheeb knew the woman to be Heleina, Bach's ancient love.

Thunderous clouds, black with rain, rolled in from the north as patches of starlight drifted down from deepest space. Off in the distance Sheeb could see a cathedral, its gothic tower reaching up into the tempestuous night. Without knowing how, Sheeb knew that Bach was inside, the pilgrimage to Bach's cathedral taking him through valleys where streams reflected low-hung clouds mixed with starlight. Walking up to the door of the church, Sheeb heard the sound of a pipe organ echoing within the ancient hall, the music sounding strangely familiar.

Opening the large wooden door, Sheeb stepped inside and looked for Bach. He was sitting in one of the pews, tears streaming down his face as he looked up at the large stained-glass window behind the altar. The light nearly blinded Sheeb but, shielding his eyes, he could see that the window depicted the Virgin Mary, her arms held out, suspended in space with an eternal embrace.

Sheeb sat down in the pew next to Bach and looked around. There was no one else present, just the organist surrounded by massive pipes of brass and silver. It was then that Sheeb recognized the music. It was Bach! The "Fugue in F-sharp Minor" thundered against the walls of the church.

"Why are you here?" Sheeb asked.

"It's the only safe place left." Bach turned and looked at Sheeb. "Have you been outside?"

"Yes."

"Then you know what I mean." Bach sighed, seeming to drink in the light that flooded in from the figure of the Virgin. Still looking at the Madonna cast in glass, Bach raised a hand to his chin.

"So what happened with the Mind War Machine?"

Sheeb described Vollen's disappearance, Ran's death, and the altercation with Buchner and Darkos.

"Do you have the cube?" Bach interrupted.

"There is no cube."

"What do you mean?" Bach asked.

Sheeb explained how it had disintegrated during the translation and had been reborn as a star in another universe. The theories and concerns about the translation of the cube affecting this world were unfounded. The cube and the danger it posed no longer existed.

"Thank God," Bach said.

The church fell silent as the organist's great fugue came to an end. Sheeb watched him pack up his things, his bearing and looks reminding Sheeb of drawings he had seen of the baroque composer himself.

"You know," Sheeb offered, "the organist looks remarkably like Johann Sebastian Bach."

"I guess so." A slight grin slid across Bach's face.

"I don't understand," Sheeb said.

Bach waved him silent. "It's in the DNA."

"DNA?" Sheeb asked perplexed.

"Yes, Sheeb, DNA. Things are more connected than I realized...I feel myself..." Bach covered his face with his hands for a moment and then took a breath of air. "I can feel myself dying. I can feel neurons turning off. But as parts of me slip away, I am becoming aware of things I never suspected. I can feel my own DNA, Sheeb. Everything I ever experienced ... everything my ancestors ever experienced is spiraled up inside of me."

Bach leaned back in his pew. "So this cathedral is the image of a church in which my ancestor Johann played the organ, placed here in this valley of my death. The images are real. They really happened. They're just 500 years out of time. And there's something else,"

Bach looked up at the stained glass window. "I have this very odd feeling about Heleina. I feel that she is coming to meet me, as if she has never really died...just entombed in the marble of my own disbelief." Bach stared off into space and then shook his head. "But enough of this nonsense. I need you to do something."

"Of course," Sheeb responded.

"I am assuming that they have put me in my office as I requested. Am I correct?"

"Yes, Alfred."

"I want you to go to my desk and pull out the computer and punch in my personal security access code Fugue One. I then want you to issue a command to disband the Mind War Project. The computer will make it look as if I gave the order a few days before my operation. At your command, BioTech's internal security will fly out there and dismantle the entire project and destroy the records. It will be as if the Mind War Project had never existed. Let's get this madness over with."

"Will you still be in here when I'm finished?" Sheeb asked.

"Most likely. I'm certainly not going to go outside." Bach turned to face the Virgin Mary and closed his eyes.

Sheeb pulled himself out of sync, the sound of the wind outside the cathedral giving way to the murmur of oxygen pumps in Bach's office. Sheeb got up and walked over to Bach's desk. The computer commands to dismantle the Mind War Machine took only a few moments. Sheeb slid Bach's computer back into its cradle, giving the illusion that it hadn't been touched.

Back at the cube holding Bach's brain, Sheeb knelt on the floor and took a breath. In the next moment he found himself, once again, in front of the cathedral. The patches of starlight he had seen earlier were now gone. All was darkness. An eerie silence had spread over the dark valley, swallowing everything in its path. Sheeb knew he must get inside. He ran to the large wooden door, catching a glimpse of the marble statue before he slipped inside. She was still tumbling through the dark air, but her arms were free and waving like wings. The stone about her body was crumbling away, and the most mysterious smile came onto her lips as she looked into Sheeb's eyes.

He closed the door behind him. Bach was still enraptured by the light that was flooding into the church through the stained glass window of the Virgin Mary. But where was the light coming from? Outside was darkest night.

Sheeb had just stepped up to Bach's pew when the massive window shattered. Thousands of bits of glass avalanched onto the altar, the Virgin suddenly consumed by an explosion of light. Sheeb looked up. There, where the Virgin had been, in the starlight night of space, Heleina stood floating, her arms reaching out for Bach. Behind her, billions of stars began to swirl, and the light twisted itself into a tunnel that stretched out into infinity.

Bach let go of the pew and started to float in the air like a cloud, his arms outstretched into the effulgent light that now flooded the great hall. As Bach entered the tunnel of light, the two lovers embraced. In a flash of light they were gone, and only the gaping hole where the Virgin had been remained. Dark mist began to swirl into the church through the shattered window, and as Sheeb headed for the doorway the images began to blur. Bach's brain was dying, and his world of dreams was unraveling.

Pulling himself out of sync, Sheeb raised himself from the floor in front of Bach's dying brain.

Monitors screeched their anguished cry. Marc ran into the room.

The great Quasar was gone.

CHAPTER THIRTY-THREE

$\int$heeb left Bach's office just as a rainbow formed in the skies over Bethesda. He gazed at the ephemeral display for several minutes before hailing a cab for the shuttle port. Although Centauri was inordinately affectionate, Sheeb's thoughts were with Kathrina. Soon they would be together again, and the horrors of the last few days would be behind him.

Alpha Lyra skimmed over a restless sea as it headed for the small island of Christos. The onboard computer had picked up a weather alert from one of the orbiting satellites. A tropical storm northeast of the island was being upgraded to a hurricane.

Making his final approach, he caught sight of the crystal spire of the healing chamber and the canals for the Precious Ones that led out to the sea as he approached the island.

As the shuttle slowed down for docking, Sheeb noticed Kathrina on the floating pier. The sight of her filled him with excitement as he eased Alpha Lyra into the turquoise lagoon. The door to the craft opened and Sheeb stepped out onto the dock, Centauri close behind and wagging his tail furiously. The dog jumped up onto his two hind legs, front legs pawing the air, and walked three steps into Kathrina's open arms. The sound of her laughter and Centauri's barks filled the air.

Sheeb stepped up and gave Kathrina a kiss, sliding his arms up from behind and pulling her to him. Kathrina took his hand. "Come on, I want to show you something." Sheeb followed her and Centauri up the winding path toward a hill, the highest point on Christos. The harsh light of late afternoon had turned a muted gold as the sun neared the horizon. As they climbed their way to the top of the hill, pink orchids seemed to pulsate and burst into flame as the light from the setting sun turned red-orange.

"Quickly!" Kathrina spoke, tugging at Sheeb's hand. "We haven't got much time."

"Time for what?" Sheeb asked.

"You'll see." Kathrina looked back grinning, her eyes intoxicated.

As they stepped into the small clearing at the top of the hill, Kathrina threw her arms out into the air and yelled "Look!" Her right hand pointed toward the west and the setting sun as her left hand stretched east toward the rising moon, full and pregnant with a silvery light.

Sheeb felt himself take a breath as the impact of the scene hit him. As in some perfectly timed ballet, the moon rose into the night air just as the sun slipped behind the edge of earth's horizon and into the cover of darkness. The air turned mysterious with an ancient and portentous power as if both the sun and moon had just been unsealed.

"It only happens twice a year," Kathrina said excitedly. "Isn't it incredible?"

Sheeb nodded as he looked at the strange astronomical event. And then he remembered a manuscript

he had read during his college days, a six-hundred-year-old trea-
tise written by some obscure medieval alchemist. The sage had
scribbled his notes on parchment that had only recently been
unearthed in Italy. The manuscript described a mystical and
sacred marriage. But this marriage was not between the outer
man and woman. It occurred inside one's own body, between
two energies that the alchemist referred to as the sun and moon.
At the bottom of the text, an illuminated drawing revealed a
man holding the sun and a woman holding the moon. Beneath
them were stars, and they were joined like Siamese twins.
According to the author of the text, this secret union could only
occur within one who had been prepared through the fiery path
of alchemy, where opposites are resolved into one. The pressure
of such a task would birth an "inner elixir," and to such a one,
the secrets of the cosmos would be laid open.

Sheeb had dismissed the man's
ideas as fantasy, but standing now on top of the hill looking at the
sun and moon, he didn't know. He seemed possessed by unearthly
feelings, and they reminded him of his experience with the dolphins in the healing chamber. Sheeb turned toward Kathrina who
now seemed oddly detached and intoxicated.

"Kat?"

"Yes?" Kathrina's hand waved the air toward Sheeb, a
strangely soft gesture like swans in dreams.

"Where's Remeira?"

"Gone." Kathrina stared at a small boulder at the edge of
the hill.

"What do you mean, gone?" Sheeb asked.

"Just what I said." Kathrina sighed. "We had a...
disagreement."

"About what?" Sheeb asked.

"Look." Kathrina looked him straight in the eyes. "I can't put her reasons for leaving into a linear logic that you would appreciate. Besides, it has to do with Luna, which you have made clear is a mere piece of fantasy." Kathrina turned away and looked out at the moon as it was being swallowed by low clouds that were blowing in from the northeast.

Sheeb walked over and touched her on the shoulders. "We need to talk," he said. Sheeb sat on the ground and picked up a small pebble, tossing it in the air. Kathrina sat a few feet away staring at a grain of sand.

Kathrina listened intently as Sheeb recounted the events of the last few days, the death of Ran, the mysterious metamorphosis of the carbonite cube, his experience with Ran's new world, and the loss of Bach.

The sky was growing more menacing as wind-swept clouds, torn from the horizon, whipped into a frenzy above them. Kathrina sighed and looked out to sea. "I am sorry for your loss, Sheeb. There are awesome forces in this universe, forces greater than you or I will ever fathom." Kathrina looked up toward the dark sky now turning black. "There are powers that kill and powers that heal. We are a part of them all."

The moon suddenly flew out from behind a dark cloud into a clear patch of night sky, flooding the hill with a brilliant silver light. Kathrina's body began to radiate the same alabaster light that poured down from the moon above. Then she was gone, and in her place the goddess sat serenely in front of Sheeb in silence. But this was a form he hadn't seen before. There were no arms writhing like serpents, only a soft light enfolding him from her heart.

Sheeb started to speak, but the goddess waved him silent. "At first light...out on the beach...here in the calm of this storm...I will call you."

The air crashed in on itself as a bolt of lightning arced from the sky and hit a dead tree not ten feet away. Splinters and burning ash flew everywhere, the ancient oak reduced to flame and smoke. In the flash of light Sheeb could see that the goddess had left. Grabbing Kathrina's hand, he pulled her from the avalanche of burning debris that was falling into the clearing. The sweet smell of falling rain filled the air, and embers hissed as thousands of flaming stars went out on the wet earth.

The storm ripped into the island, and the gentle rain turned into a torrent, sending Sheeb and Kathrina down the hill toward the cottage, Centauri following close behind. They were soaking wet. Pulling off their clothes in the foyer, Kathrina kissed Sheeb on the lips and then ran up the spiral stairs toward her bedroom. The sound of thunder shook the room and streams of water flowed across the floor through the open windows. Sheeb looked up and caught a glimpse of Kathrina's naked back as she slipped into the upstairs hallway. He wanted her. He could taste her in his mouth.

Bolting up the stairs, Sheeb ran into the hallway. A flash of lightning lit the house, and Sheeb could see Kathrina standing by her bed toweling herself. The room went dark, and then the feel of flesh against flesh as he slipped up beside her. A faint gasp of pleasure passed her lips as he lifted her and lowered her still-moist body onto satin sheets.

Kathrina bit his shoulder, and pressing her arms against the bed, arched her back, a shudder rippling through her thighs and up into her belly. A bolt of lightning lit the frenzied sky and then the blast of exploding thunder rocked the room again. The smell of ozone mixed with rain drifted in the air.

Burying his face into Kathrina's rich auburn hair left Sheeb intoxicated. He raised his head for air, the rich sea of smells from the swirling ocean pulling him deeper into ecstasy. He felt the fingers of Kathrina's hand pulling at his sex, calling him inside her. In his mind, a giant eel slid past him and down into a watery canyon as whispers of pleasure washed over him.

It felt as if they had passed into the ocean, into a world of water. Almost delirious from passion, Sheeb thought he heard dolphins. Surely Shiva and Shakti must be in the bathtub next door. Streams of water flowing across the floor had turned into a river, and reaching down, Kathrina slid her fingers through the torrent and slipped her wet fingers into Sheeb's mouth.

Sheeb grinned and slid her underneath him. His muscles quivered. Dendrites and synapses exploded with pleasure-electricity. A sheet of lightning ignited directly overhead.

Sheeb felt his throat, heart, and gut opening. A hundred million sperm swam hysterically from the rich milkiness of their sea into Kathrina's warm and pulsating womb. The two lovers lay entwined together for the longest time, and then rolling onto his side, Sheeb pulled Kathrina close to him. Outside, the moon was rising through clouds, casting her silvery light over a still restless sea. Languid with pleasure and exhausted from the last several days, Sheeb slipped a hand beneath his head and fell asleep.

Moonbeam, mixed with sea breeze, cascaded into the room through open curtains. Kathrina rose from the bed and walked to the window. Raising a hand to her belly, Kathrina felt something stirring within. One of her eggs had slipped from its fallopian harbor into the vast intrauterine sea. Off in the distance, across the ocean, Kathrina could sense millions of sperm swimming in the cross currents of her womb.

As they neared the egg, invisible fingers of energy reached out into the murky sea, touching galaxies of sperm, searching them...testing each member of the swimming flotilla, as if the egg was fathoming the genetic matrix of each excited visitor. The outer walls of the egg quivered from the impact of several dozen sperm, but the egg only opened her molecular door to one of them. Swimming past the closing portal, the lone sperm entered the inner temple and poured its DNA into the pulsing center of the egg. Like dandelion seed blown on the wind, the sperm surrendered its genetic matrix to the waiting orb.

Kathrina watched for some time as the egg within her merged the strands of her own DNA with the matrix of Sheeb's sperm. Even now, as Sheeb slept, the egg had started to divide.

Looking at Sheeb nestled in her sheets, Kathrina felt her heart opening with a great love for him. For a moment she just stood there, watching the rising and falling of his breathing. She yearned to walk over and kiss his belly, the palms of his hands...his forehead, yes...his forehead, where his sixth chakra was opening like a rose. She could see it. She had seen it before in her students when they first began to see the new world of light and vibration...a world which no one could enter and return from unchanged.

Kathrina knew that she could never know the anguish and pressure within her lover that had driven the opening. She could only guess at it, drawing from her own dark nights when the goddess had first appeared to her.

Kathrina let the love from her heart float out across the room to Sheeb, the soft pink light filtering down around him like a pastel cocoon. The release of love always left Kathrina in ecstasy, and leaning against the wall, Kathrina let herself float in the feelings for a while. But the pleasurable sensations abruptly ended.

A cold knife-like feeling pulled Kathrina's awareness to the ocean. Standing there by the open window, Kathrina looked out beyond the coral reef that protected Christos from the angry sea. They were coming. She could feel their darkness. There were three men and a woman. They did not know nor did they care about the New World. Love did not exist for them, only power.

Kathrina sighed and let the disturbing vision subside. If she was to survive, she would have to call upon everything she had ever learned. Feeling cold and alone, Kathrina slipped into bed beside Sheeb and slid her arm around his side and across his belly. The softness of his breath was comforting, and cuddling up against him, she drifted off to sleep.

CHAPTER THIRTY-FOUR

 $\int$ till asleep, Sheeb rolled over onto his side. Kathrina's arm slid across his waist and dropped to the sheets, finally resting like a seashell against the small of his back. Outside... the swelling ocean had come to rest. The island had entered the eye of the storm, and an eerie silence hovered in the air.

The dark sky had parted into chunks of floating cloud, and the moon, drifting soundlessly through starlight, bathed everything in her silvery brilliance. Sheeb's head turned toward the moonlight, the mercurial light enfolding him, and in his dreaming mind everything turned silver.

He was walking down a metal corridor, a silvery light flooding the hallway through an open door. Walking toward the light, Sheeb passed into a large chamber. "My god!" The words blurted out through Sheeb's lips. He had stumbled into the hiberdome of the Plutonian Explorer. The crew of the expedition lay sleeping in their hibernation tanks, the seven members, four men and three women clearly visible behind plastishield.

Sheeb wandered around the large circle that their tanks inscribed inside the chamber. The crew had been chosen for their genetic excellence—combinations of genius and physical perfection. Culled from the finest of humanity's gene pool, they now slept in a frozen slumber, unaware of their deathly fate.

Sheeb walked over to one of the windows that looked out into the starlit darkness of deep space. Somewhere behind them, among the spirals of gas and asteroids, Earth rotated around the sun in her great elliptical orbit. What was it that had propelled these men and women to the edge of the solar system? And what was it about the edge of things that drew men as surely as moths are drawn to flame?

The ill-fated crew was careening past Pluto into deepest space. And in that moment, the Greek god of the underworld seemed to be quite real. An insidious feeling had clung to Sheeb's dream-mind as soon as he entered the Plutonian Explorer. Looking at the members of the doomed expedition, Sheeb felt himself getting drowsy as if some strange power was pulling him into that same eternal sleep. But fight it he must. To give in to the seductive temptation of slumber would be to surrender the hard-won victory of consciousness itself.

In the moment of his dreaming, it felt as if the future history of humanity depended upon whether he could stay awake or not. The impression became even more vivid as the Explorer passed through the shadowy fingers of Pluto's orbit. The electrical patterns within Sheeb's brain quivered with the impact of this realization, and his dream turned lucid. "How odd!" Sheeb thought to himself.

He knew that he was dreaming, and even more, he suddenly understood that he and all of mankind believed themselves to be awake when they were really but awash in dream. The triumphs and tragedies of human history had been nothing more than dreams dreamt within the boundless ocean of infinite space. Mankind never realized the awful secret of their own minds—that in the dark shadowlands of their subconscious there lived a power that wanted only to kill, to wound and to destroy. It cared for nothing else, and like the Sirens of ancient Greece, it had an alluring and seductive power. It called out to all humans, no matter how great or small, and with its ancient powers, lulled them into the unconscious madness of self-destruction. It was this same horrible power, living in every man and woman, that had birthed the Inquisition, the Holocaust, and all the dark ravages of human history. It lived in the shadows of the human mind. It could, with one twist of its powers, ruin friendships, mar the face of history, destroy whole nations, and lay waste the kinder and more gentle natures of man.

Sheeb felt the dark power pulling at him...seducing him into unconsciousness. If he succumbed, he would never be able to re-awaken. He knew this with every cell of his body. His mind filled with static as he fought the power for every last shred of awareness. The room turned brittle like glass. As Sheeb fell to the floor with fatigue, he heard a voice over the radio, faint yet somehow strangely familiar.

"Wake up!"

The voice crackled through the static of cosmic dust. "Wake up, dammit!"

Sheeb dragged himself from the floor and staggered over to the console. His hand grabbed the mike and pulled it to his mouth. "Who are you?" he asked. For a moment there was only silence and the slush of electromagnetic disturbance...then laugher. Sheeb shuddered as he recognized the voice. "Ran?"

"Yes, Sheeb."

"Is that you?"

The radio crackled with howling laughter and Sheeb awakened from his dream. His eyes popped open and the world flashed silver for a moment. Outside, the moon lay still and silent against a patch of starlight. Sheeb sighed and rolled away from Kathrina.

Rising to his feet, Sheeb walked to the window that opened to the sea. In the hushed air, he could hear the wind, not far off, shredding cloud and water, but here on the island, all was still. Below, the beach stretched out like white marble into a strangely quiet and dark sea.

Sheeb was thinking about the mysterious dream when he felt the goddess calling him—calling him to the edge of the island, her whisperings borne to him on sea breeze and moonbeam.

Kathrina lay still sleeping. Sheeb kissed her on the temple, her breath soft like butterflies in twilight. Outside, the air pulsed pregnant with aromas from the sea. The storm had ripped algae and creatures from the waters onto the shore, a rich salty perfume everywhere. Off in the distance, storm clouds circled the island.

Falling to his knees out on the beach, Sheeb sat back on his haunches. Foamy fingers of seawater pulled at him. Above, the moon lay floating in a patch of clear sky. Shreds of cloud wisped into tendrils of mist around the silver orb.

"So...you have come to meet me." The goddess spoke to him, it seemed from inside his mind.

"Yes. You promised me knowledge."

The goddess laughed, a soft edge to her voice.

"Why don't you show yourself to me like you did the last time?" Sheeb asked.

"I am everywhere, and I do not desire to limit my form for you at this moment."

"I don't understand how you can be everywhere," Sheeb said.

"That's because your mind is too small."

"So what should I do?" Sheeb asked.

"See the circle that the horizon is making around you?" the goddess asked.

"Yes." The whole island seemed surrounded by a dark curtain of clouds hugging the horizon.

"Now imagine that your skull extends out to the horizon, and everything you see... even the moon... is inside your head. Let your mind expand past its boundaries."

Sheeb let his awareness roll out to the distant clouds. His eyes rolled back in their sockets as he felt the imaginary boundary of his skull shifting out to the wall of rain and cloud. Suddenly the world snapped. His body quivered for a moment as heat rocketed up from the base of his spine into his reeling brain. Synapses sparked with the surge of neural electricity. Sheeb opened his eyes. Everything had turned translucent, and it felt to him, sitting on the beach, as if the entire world was inside his head.

The goddess suddenly appeared in front of him, her thousand hands swaying in the silvery moonlight. "You asked for knowledge," she said. "You, of course, thought it would be another mental concept... an abstract plaything to mull over in your mind." A slight smile of amusement parted the goddess's lips. "But that is not the knowledge of which I speak." One of the deity's hands rose from her side and snapped its fingers. A bolt of lightning shot out from her luminous form and struck Sheeb at the crown of his head.

Sheeb jerked from the sudden impact. The top of his head ached, and his body was rocking in small circles. A few yards in front of him, a school of flying fish did acrobatics on the silverlit surface of the water.

Although he could not see it, he could still sense it. There was a strange power in the air, but what was it? It pulsed in the air, spinning around him. It quivered inside his blood and in every cell of his body. It hummed inside the smallest atom. Wherever he looked, everything shimmered with an exquisite beauty. Sheeb looked down to his hands. The power was pulsing into his arms, pulsing with every beat of his heart.

Dolphins taking refuge from the storm in the open waters off the island nuzzled each other with the same power that spiraled itself into Sheeb's blood. Far beyond the horizon, Sheeb could sense Europe as clearly as if he were standing there himself. Fishermen off the coast of Gaul pulled their nets from the bristling sea. The strange power surged into their arms, biceps shaking from the weight of heavy nets. And in the netting, a thousand fish wrestled against certain death with the same power that pulled them onto the wooden boats.

In Madrid, the sun was rising. And on the floor of a third story loft, two lovers were awakened by the warmth of sunlight as it streamed through their open window. The young man, aroused with the exquisite ache of morning passion, reached for his beloved. And it was the same power... the same power within their passion that drove the sun to rise, and the same power that fired the great star with explosions of helium and hydrogen gas.

To Sheeb, it felt as if the power was shaking matter at its very roots, shaking it as if trying to awaken something, but what? The power seemed to pulse from everything, even the rocks at his feet.

"It comes from everywhere," the goddess said, sensing Sheeb's quandary. "It has been calling you from your farthest future, and it is calling you from your most distant past. It cannot be contained. It has a mind of its own, it wants some-thing, and it wants you to know it."

"Know what?" Sheeb asked.

"It's time for the monkeys to wake up. You've all been sleeping long enough."

"Wake up to what?" Sheeb asked.

"To your power!" the goddess bellowed.

"But," Sheeb protested, "you said my mind was too small."

The goddess laughed. "You are not your mind, Sheeb. You are nowhere near what or who you think yourself to be. You are, how shall I put this—a speck of cosmic dust, an evolu-tionary fluke, and yet... the power of the entire universe lies hidden inside your monkey mind. When your species discovers this truth, your collective destiny will forever be changed."

Sheeb began to ask something, but Luna snapped her fingers and was gone. His audience was over. Stunned by his experience with the goddess, Sheeb returned to the cottage and Kathrina.

CHAPTER THIRTY-FIVE

"Damn!" the urgency of Torn's cursing echoed off the air-transport's aluminum walls as the small craft shuddered in the hail of wind and water. Beneath them, Christos slipped in and out of cloud tendrils that had been ripped across the sky.

Buchner yelled to his pilot above the deafening roar of the storm. "Torn get us down!"

"I'm trying, Mr. Buchner, I'm trying."

Torn nosed the craft toward the tiny island, the fury of the wind pushing back against him. The thick muscles of his arms were aching from the pressure of holding the shuttle on course. Finally, he managed to lower the shuttle toward the maddening sea and the circle of coral that protected the refuge of Christos.

Buchner peered down through the small port window at his side. It was a habit of his to congratulate himself whenever he did anything that was particularly outstanding. And certainly his plan to bug Sheeb's shuttle with a homing device after the ill-fated assassination attempt fell into that category. In moments they would be on the island, and then Sheeb would pay for his pathetic escape with his very mind. And if there was any trace of information about the

Mind War Machine secreted away within his brain, the Deep Mind Probe would rip it from him.

Kathrina looked over at Sheeb, his eyes closed, deep in trance. The wind was furling the white curtains by the windows over and over like clouds that had been tethered to the wall. She spoke softly against the wail of the storm outside, trying to envelop Sheeb in stillness.

"What do you see?" she asked.

Sheeb turned his head slightly, as if gazing at something, "I see Buchner looking down at the island." A wave of anger swept through Sheeb's mind, and his fist hit the carpet. "That bastard!"

Kathrina's hand gently touched his leg, but with an urgency that could not be escaped. "If you indulge yourself, you'll kill us both."

Sheeb nodded. Kathrina was right. It would take poise and balance to win this time. The four mind thieves were heavily armed with lasers, sound impulsers (weapons which stunned or killed their victims with sound frequencies), and Parasympths. Parasympth gas was used to paralyze. One whiff of the orderless vapor would overactivate the parasympathetic nervous system leaving its victim's mind in tact while paralyzing most of the body's major muscles. How clever and cruel of Buchner to think of it!

Kathrina urged him on. "What else?"

"They're almost here."

Kathrina nodded. "How far?"

"About two miles, and twelve hundred feet in altitude."

Kathrina touched Sheeb's thigh again. "Good. Now my love, tell me what you feel?"

"What do you mean?" Sheeb asked perplexedly.

"When you see him in your mind, tell me what you feel in your heart." Kathrina was testing him for his accuracy of psychic impressions. Their lives might very well depend on it.

Sheeb paused, and then spoke as a sheet of mist was hurled across the room through the open window. "I feel that they...that they are isolated. There is no connection between them. Yes!" Sheeb exclaimed excitedly. "I see what you mean."

"And Sheeb," Kathrina's voice sounded full with satisfaction "that's what allowed you to escape them—their disconnection and your bonding with Centauri."

Centauri sat up beside Sheeb and made a soft noise at the back of his throat. Sheeb stroked the dog's head. "Kat, I'm feeling you in a way I've never felt before." By now Sheeb had entered the telepathic web that had been woven between them, and the weft and weave of her thoughts were instantly sewn into his mind.

Kathrina answered him in silence, her words clear as crystal. And with every word there were colors that swirled before him. How beautiful, he thought, the colors of Kathrina's voice to be.

"My love...." The colors of her voice turned to a deep resonant pink. "We must bond together..... the three of us."

"That's our only hope isn't it.... to move with the same mind." Sheeb asked.

Kathrina reached over and touched Sheeb once again. "Yes."

Sheeb slowly opened his eyes and looked at his lover. Her eyes glistened. Sheeb could taste the salty sweetness of the sea on his tongue. Everything seemed amplified. There was an awesome power to the moment. And although the air outside was exploding with the fury of the storm, everything felt calm and peaceful inside. A strange silence pervaded the room.

Centauri nuzzled up to the two of them, and both Sheeb and Kathrina put their arms around the animal. For a moment, they just sat there gazing into each other's eyes. And then as if magnets were pulling their eyes shut, the three of them turned inward.

Beneath them the Earth rolled on its axis like a ball around the sun. The stars of other worlds lay strewn off in the distance like luminous stones. And to their left, the moon was hovering in all her silver splendor.

Ribbons of light were streaming from each of their hearts to the other, and Sheeb felt the deepness of their love for him swirling into every cell of his body. The force of their love shook free a long-forgotten sadness. In the distance, a little boy was crying. Sheeb could see him against the backdrop of starlight. To feel unloved is a most terrible thing, and in the depth of Kathrina's and Centauri's love, Sheeb's wounding was being plowed under.

Sheeb felt the seeds of something new sprouting in his head, the roots reaching down into his heart. The top of his head ached, and from the opening at his crown a sunflower unfurled itself into the womb of interstellar space.

Sheeb opened his eyes. Kathrina and Centauri were still in trance. Funny, but Sheeb could see the room around him, and still "see" the three of them floating together above the Earth; and he could still feel the sunflower in his mind swaying in the solar stream that issued from Earth's great star.

Kathrina opened her eyes and looked into Sheeb. Centauri opened his eyes and looked at the two of them. Throwing back his head, the animal howled, reminding Sheeb of the coyotes he had heard out on the New Mexico desert.

"There's not much time left." Sheeb spoke telepathically.

Kathrina nodded. The Mind Thieves had landed on the south side of the island, their shuttle hidden amidst the mango trees.

Torn was the first to emerge from the shuttle. The torrent of rain had pulled some trees down, their knotted roots wet and twisting into the air. The motor pool driver, Jeff, was next, and pulling the canisters of Parasympth back against his sides, he motioned to the others. Buchner pulled a parka over his head as he followed Torn. Darkos stepped behind Buchner, and cursed the air beneath her breath. The entire affair had become more complicated than she had planned, and even if they found Sheeb, she no longer trusted Buchner to be fair with her.

The narrow path snaked back in on itself as it rose to the top of a small clearing that overlooked the compound. In the torrent of rain, Torn could just barely make out the buildings. And then the storm quieted, the island turning oddly still. The moon slipped out from behind clouds, and the darkness gave way to a silvery light.

"This way!" Torn motioned, and walked down the path toward the main building.

From the balcony, Sheeb had been watching the trail. In his hands he held the only weapon on the island—a Stellar Optic Laser. The rifle-like gun was used for target practice. Designed to shoot floating aluminum, the laser emitted a thin beam of light, intense and highly accurate.

Looking intently through the infrared telescope, Sheeb spotted Torn as he emerged from the bushes. The terminator turned to speak to Buchner, and the transport driver from the Bosk mansion stepped forward into the moonlit clearing.

"Just a little bit closer, fuckhead." Sheeb whispered.

Sheeb aimed the laser at the canister of Parsympth that had just slipped over the man's belly. With any luck, Sheeb thought, the arc of light would rip into his stomach when it pierced the aluminum canister. The air snapped with the high-pitched whine of the Stellar Optic, and Jeff moaned as the light slit open the canister of gas. Grabbing his stomach, he doubled over in pain as the burning light burrowed itself into his gut.

Torn grabbed his gas mask and yelled at the others before pulling it over his face. Darkos and Buchner slipped their masks on just as clouds of Parasympth exploded into the air. Jeff's legs started to shake uncontrollably, and falling to the ground, he peed on himself. His body spasmed and lay sprawled out on the wet earth, suddenly worthless. Torn cursed and ran back into the underbrush where Buchner and Darkos were waiting.

"What now?" Buchner asked.

"We go around to the side...there." Torn pointed to a dense planting of dwarf orange trees that pushed up against the house.

Buchner nodded. Torn led the way back around the house. Darkos turned back to look at Jeff stretched out on the ground. A small stream of dirt and water had backed up against his side, swirling down around his legs and over his feet.

Sheeb checked the Stellar Optic. After he shot Jeff, the gun had emitted a malfunction alert. The rain must have short-circuited the fragile instrument. Slipping back inside, Sheeb placed the rifle against the wall and took the towel that Kathrina held out for him. As he raised the towel to his head, Kathrina nodded toward the side of the house where Torn, Buchner, and Darkos were heading.

"Yes," Sheeb said telepathically. He now understood what Ran had said about the energy it took to talk. It was so much easier to communicate without speaking.

Kathrina headed for the side of the house encircled by the dwarf orange trees. Centauri padded his way behind her, and Sheeb, tossing the towel onto the floor, followed them downstairs into the large temple room. One whole wall was lined with glass doors opened to the patio, the smell of rain and ripe oranges wafting into the room.

Silently crossing the room, Kathrina bowed before the low altar where a single flame burned in an oil lamp. "The votive symbolizes the light of truth that reflects itself through all spiritual traditions," Kathrina telepathed silently to Sheeb. She had felt his questions about the altar.

All along the other two sides of the room, various forms of the goddess were lined up against the walls: Kali, the goddess of destruction; Kuan Yin, the goddess of compassion; Isis, the Egyptian mother goddess and her sister, Hathor, goddess of fertility and sexual bliss. Finally a statue of Saraswati, goddess of the arts and sciences sat next to a figure of Mary, the mother of Jeshua. The revered feminine deities from throughout the world had been lovingly ensconced within the great chamber. A candle sat burning in front of each figure, and the effect of so many candles was to cast the room into a mysterious golden light.

Kathrina turned to Sheeb. The Mind Thieves were closer. She could "see" them crawling their way around the trees to the stone terrace just outside. "We will wait here," Kathrina telepathed. Sheeb nodded and hid in the shadows of Isis while Kathrina slipped behind the giant carving of Kali. Centauri crept across the floor to sit at the edge of the altar.

Through the web of their *seeing* all three of them were able to follow Buchner, Darkos, and Torn. In minutes, they would be at the door to the altar room. Kathrina's hand idly stroked the back of the Wrathful Mother. Was it destruction that was needed now, or was it compassion? Kathrina looked across the room to the serene figure of Kuan Yin, and her ever-compassionate eyes, but her reverie was broken by Centauri's growl. The deadly visitors had arrived.

"Quiet!" Sheeb telepathed.

Centauri relaxed, his eyes still riveted on the door. Crouched behind the Egyptian goddess, Sheeb could clearly see Torn slinking across the stone terrace toward the opened doors. Buchner and Darkos were close behind. As Torn stepped into the darkened room of relics, he raised a hand to his eyes, the blue of them flickering in the warm glow of candle.

The room blurred as Centauri bolted for the intruder. Torn screamed in agony and outrage as the dog ripped into his arm. Rivers of blood poured down onto hard stone.

Sheeb whirled from behind the massive statue of Isis and ran outside onto the terrace. As if it had been choreographed and rehearsed a thousand times, Kathrina leapt into the air behind her love, the sudden vision of them startling Buchner and Darkos. The air exploded with thunder, and an avalanche of rain began to pour from a tempestuous sky.

In the sudden confusion, Sheeb knocked Buchner unconscious, and Kathrina wrestled the female assassin to the ground. Darkos bellowed as her arm crashed into the solid granite of the floor. Her laser fell loose from her hand and Kathrina reached for it in the torrent of rain. Darkos pulled at her blouse, and yanking her back, grabbed her neck and started to choke her. So this was the darkness that Luna had brought to her.

Kathrina shrieked in outrage, and threw Darkos around, slamming her head into the leg of a wrought iron chair. For a moment, the woman was stunned, but returning to her senses, she clawed at her would-be captor.

"Why?" Kathrina asked. "Why do you want to do this?"

Darkos struggled to get free, but Kathrina would not let go. She lay on top of the woman, pressing her arms against the wet stone. Darkos hissed, and twisting like a reptile, she spun around and bit Kathrina in the left breast. Kathrina screamed and slapped Darkos in the face, drawing blood from the force of the impact.

Buchner lay moaning on the terrace floor. Turning his attention to the avalanche of glass and blood by the doorway, Sheeb noticed Centauri lying in a puddle of water and blood, panting. Torn had kicked him in the chest when the dog had first attacked.

Sheeb crouched and turned toward Torn. The terminator reached down and grabbed his laser that had fallen into a pile of splintered glass.

"Hold it!" Torn bellowed. He rocked back and forth on his heels, blood dripping from the same hand that Centauri had ripped open at the Bosk mansion. For just a moment, time seemed to still itself, and Sheeb watched as vermilion drops of fluid dripped from Torn's fingers. Shimmering, each droplet of blood quivered with the essence of life itself. How odd and magnificent it seemed, in that instant, to watch Torn bleeding in the midst of oranges!

Sheeb had never felt like this before. The freedom was intoxicating. It seemed as if he could feel and touch every molecule and atom with the power of his mind. Sheeb could sense Centauri's pain, but in some extraordinary way it didn't matter. The rib was not broken, just a slight hair-line fracture. The dog would be fine. Sheeb felt a love for both dog and the man who had hurt him. How odd, not to feel fear.

Looking down at Darkos, Kathrina suddenly remembered Luna's words to her only days before: "You must love as the great stream loves." And suddenly Kathrina's heart was filled with love for her would-be destroyer. Only moments before, Kathrina wanted to crush her. Now she only wished to forgive. The great paradox of destruction and compassion had been resolved in Kathrina's mind. Kathrina let Darkos free, and slowly standing, she said, "I will not harm you."

Darkos seemed confused, and in a panic she slid herself across the floor to Buchner, who had just stood up.

Sheeb felt the power of Kathrina's action. It was as if an extraordinary mantle of protection had fallen over them, and nothing, it seemed, could touch them. He started to walk toward his beloved.

"Stop!" Torn screamed, the air tremoring from the onslaught of his rage. "Stop or I'll kill him!" Torn turned the laser on Centauri, still panting and lying on the soaked stone.

Sheeb's eyes met Kathrina's and the air turned silent. For an instant they stood motionless, staring at each other, their telepathic web growing stronger. Torn sensed something between them, but couldn't figure it out. Shrugging, he aimed the laser at Centauri's eyes and pulled the trigger. In the instant that his finger squeezed the metal, Sheeb and Kathrina closed their eyes. The space around them seemed to collapse, and it felt as if they were everywhere at once. Sheeb could sense each minute change in the atoms around him. Stopping a laser was child's play.

Sheeb and Kathrina both shifted their awareness to the laser in Torn's hand. Kathrina delayed the magnetic crystal from engaging as Sheeb diverted the stream of photons back into itself. It had only taken an instant, long enough for Torn to blink and realize that something was wrong. But it was too late.

The laser screamed, and the pulse of light exploded in his hands. Torn bellowed as the swath of flame ripped into his flesh, vaporizing his arms and smelting his bones. The air was buffeted by the explosion and the ground hissed as drops of fat and muscle quivered in the cold rain.

Buchner began to shake uncontrollably, and turning, ran into the thicket of trees. For a moment, Darkos stood very still and looked at Kathrina. She started to speak, but turned and ran off behind Buchner.

Sheeb ran over to Centauri and lifted his head. Kathrina knelt down beside him, and joined her mind to his. What might have taken weeks to heal took only minutes in the highly charged energy of their joining. Centauri slowly rose from the ground and sat up. Sheeb pulled the animal to his chest.

Above them, the sky had parted to reveal the moon, still full and radiant, floating serenely in a sea of stars. Kathrina spoke silently. "They're leaving."

"Yes," Sheeb said, as he "saw" them taking off. The Mind Thieves had left the island. As Sheeb turned his attention back to Centauri for a moment, Kathrina wandered off a few steps, her eyes fixed on the moon above.

She now understood what Remeira had been saying. The power to block Torn's laser had fountained up from within her, from her own nature. And she had joined that power with Sheeb to save Centauri, themselves, and, no doubt, future human history as well.

The great work that Luna had set before her was now accomplished. Kathrina finally understood the truth of her mysterious dual nature, how goddess and woman were intertwined...and how the goddess needed the woman just as surely as the woman needed the divine.

Centauri, drawn by the shift in Kathrina's energy, grabbed Sheeb's shirt sleeve and pulled him toward her. Sheeb slipped his arms around her waist, and turning back, Kathrina kissed him on the cheek.

For the longest time, they just stood there looking at the moon and rocking from side to side. At their feet, Centauri sat looking up at the stars. Sniffing the breeze, Centauri turned his head toward the orchard. The air was rich with the smells of earth and water. For a moment he caught a whiff of something familiar, remembered from his earliest days as a puppy. Perhaps it was the smell of roots unearthed by the storm, or the exquisite freshness of the sea breeze. Whatever it was, the smell of the earth thrilled him. How wondrous and beautiful the mystery of being alive!

Centauri jumped onto his hind legs, and reaching his front paws to Sheeb and Kathrina, the three of them danced beneath starlight.

CHAPTER THIRTY-SIX

After the Mind Thieves left the island, Sheeb fell ill with a strange fever. Delirious and sweating, he thrashed in his bed for days, barely aware of this world. Kathrina watched and nursed him, understanding all too well what he was experiencing. The shock of seeing the workings of the universe so directly was burning him, literally burning the neural sheaths within his brain. There was nothing Kathrina could do but bathe him in cool water, and sing gentle lullabies to calm his fevered mind.

In his delirium, Sheeb entered his dream world so deeply that everything seemed dream-like, especially the beautiful goddess who sometimes sang to him.

He was walking along a dried river bed strewn with stars. On his back he carried a straw basket. Every few feet he would stop and retrieve tiny stars from the earth, placing them in the woven backpack. Following the river, he tracked it until it entered a large and mysterious sea. As he passed into the vast estuary, he could make out a solitary figure rowing a wooden boat toward him through the mist. As the boat with man came closer, Sheeb could make out his dear friend manning the oars.

"Hop inside," Ran said as he motioned to the empty seat up front. Sheeb got in and sat down facing Ran.

"So what were you doing?" Ran asked.

"Picking up parts of myself," Sheeb responded.

"Oh...so you realize that you're made of stars..hey?" On the word hey, Ran raised his voice high and squeaky like an old man and then slapped his naked thighs. For days and nights, it seemed, they traversed mist-shrouded waters. On the third day, Ran oared the boat to the other side of the strange sea. Beaching the boat, Ran jumped out and pulled the small vessel ashore. "There," he said. "Your future is calling you." Ran motioned Sheeb to a trail that led into a dense forest of orange trees.

Sheeb followed the trail to the edge of the trees, and then turned to speak. "Aren't you coming?" he asked. But Ran was gone. So was the fever, and Sheeb opened his eyes for the first time in almost a week. Kathrina was sleeping, her head lying on a pillow by his side. Looking at his lover, he sensed the newness of life stirring within her womb, and dropping into sync, he watched with fondness and with love the small life floating in her uterine sea.

Within that small sphere of budding life, a whole universe lay spinning on its tiny axis—a world unto itself, floating within its mother. Today his child was just a tiny zygote, untethered yet by the placental cord and hardly more significant than any other protozoan. But soon a heart would begin to beat and tiny hands and feet would sprout from its sides like the eyes on a potato. And with each pulse of its tiny heart, Sheeb could sense the same power that sprouted seeds into redwoods, that drove whales to their summer feeding grounds and had set the stars ablaze with light. And this strange and ever-present power was nothing less than the Great Mystery itself, folding and containing itself within yet another form. How magnificent to feel the pulse of love itself, unfolding and expressing itself everywhere. Love without end. Amen.

A POST SCRIPT
TO THE READER

A funny thing happened while writing this book—the world changed.

I wrote **Mind Thieves** about twenty years ago, working on it at nights and between sessions with clients in my psychotherapy practice. All in all, it took me about three and one-half years to create this imaginary futuristic world.

After my agent had been unable to find a publisher, I put the manuscript in a box and forgot about it. I also put a copy of the floppy disk in with my other word processing disks that sat on top of my desk. Moving several times in the fifteen years since I finished the book, the box mysteriously disappeared. I have no idea what happened to it. I had also forgotten about the floppy. Then one day I was cleaning up my office, which I like to do every five years or so. As I tossed old floppies into the trash, I came across the copy of **Mind Thieves**. I remember the afternoon vividly. I held the floppy between my fingers and wondered whether to toss it into the trash or not. Curious, more than anything else, I slid it into the disk drive and pulled it up on the screen. For the rest of the afternoon, I re-experienced the make-believe world I had created so long ago. After reading the manuscript, I decided to re-write small portions of it, and what you hold in your hands is the result.

It's funny to think about the world during those intervening years. When I started **Mind Thieves**, personal computers were just becoming available. After handwriting the first fourth of the book, I decided to purchase a brand new Epson. It had all of 50 megabytes! It used DOS, since Windows was still a dream, and it took up half my desk space. When I flipped it on, it hummed and vibrated like a vacuum cleaner and took several minutes to boot up. I remember the screen was luminescent green, which, back then, was one of the latest techno innovations.

In my imaginary world I created laser discs for Sheeb to view, but had no idea that they would become a reality. A few years after writing that part, CDs and DVDs came into the market place and electronic entertainment will never be the same again.

I gave Sheeb an imaginary portable phone that connected him to any part of the world via satellites. At the time, no such thing existed. Now cell phones have invaded our public and private lives in ways unimaginable twenty years ago.

I also created a line of imaginary designer drugs for my characters. I imagined that pharmaceutical companies of the future would design drugs for non-medical purposes, like entertainment and intelligence increase. I even gave these imaginary drugs names, which I had to change in the re-write because some pharmaceutical company had actually used that name for one of their drugs!

Looking at the manuscript from a futuristic angle, the only thing that hasn't been created is the Vocostrati, that strange instrument that fine tunes a musical composition to the conductor's emotions. I think we may never see such a contraption since I can't imagine an economic gain to be made by creating it. Still, of all the futuristic inventions in the book, this was the one that intrigued and still intrigues me the most.

ART, AESTHETICS, AND ILLUMINATION

One of my fascinations over the years has been the use of art and aesthetics to stimulate illumination and insight.

I still recall with awe and wonder the first time I participated in an artistic creation. I was in high school and had gone to a summer music camp directed by Dr. Lara Hogard. A consummate musician and conductor, Dr. Hogard shaped one hundred young voices into a breathtaking chorus. We performed with a professional symphony only two weeks after we had first met. The power and beauty of our performance stunned the audience as well as me. For an hour we were uplifted on wings of sound, transported to a world of beauty where magic revealed itself at every moment.

I left the concert and the inspiring presence of Dr. Hogard in a state of transcendence that lasted for several days. I had touched the power of the "muses" and I was never to be the same.

As I began to piece together the elements of my own art, whether created from sound and music or through the written word, I was guided by a desire to create beautiful experiences for my audience.

I understand that the Navajos have a term for healing that means "Returning to Beauty." I think there is great wisdom and insight in this way of viewing things. When we allow ourselves to be touched by a beautiful experience, there is a spontaneous healing or renewing energy that is released within us.

A glimpse of beauty can inspire us. The root of the word, inspire, actually means to inhale, to draw into ourselves life giving air. When we are truly inspired by something, a beautiful musical composition, an exquisite painting or dance, or a moving piece of word-craft, we naturally take a deep breath. This oxygenation of our blood has many positive benefits from a neurological perspective. From the alchemical view of consciousness, it is even more interesting for we are earthbound creatures with all of its attendant limitations. An encounter with beauty can transform us. For a moment we draw into our earthly bodies the most ephemeral of gases—air. We are joined with the heavens through the power of inspiration. This spontaneous response to beauty can set off a cascade of neurological and physiological effects that can leave us feeling unbound to Earth. Through this freeing of our bodies and minds we have the possibility for a glimpse of our transcendent and luminous natures. And this, I feel, is one of the inherent powers of great art.

Thus, I feel aligned with the ancient Hindu conception of the artist as one whose sacred task is to create harmony and beauty within society. For by creating harmony, the artist helps to protect and uplift the collective psyche of his or her people.

Art also has the possibility of engaging us in ways that create self-insight. The awareness of what ignites our passions in response to what we see or hear can be highly illuminating. And the more of ourselves we are aware of, I think, the better. Finally, I have found art in all its various forms to be a good companion on the journey of life. Good artistic expression is at the very least, entertaining. Great art can uplift us when we have stumbled and inspire us to be more than we might otherwise imagine ourselves to be.

For myself, art is a means to an end. It is a kind of bridge between the worlds. While I am creating, I am lost in the mists and luminous light of the "other realms." I am untouched by the concerns of my daily world. I am renewed. It is here, in this mysterious world of the mind, that Apollo dwells, the ancient Greek god of prophecy, music, medicine and poetry. And while I am sometimes content to simply enter this realm alone, as an artist, it is my hope that I can uncover "the gifts" of the Divine that lay strewn about us like jewels wherever we care to look.

Tom Kenyon

SOUND, MUSIC, AND CONSCIOUSNESS

Much of this novel deals with the peculiar effects of sound. There is a reason for this.

The author is also a musician. As a psychotherapist in private practice, Tom began composing music to assist his clients in the transformational process. It quickly became apparent that sound and music were powerful agents for change, and this led him to a scientific inquiry of the phenomena. Just what were the neurological and physiological reasons for these powerful changes, he asked?

A quick look at the available research on sound in the early 1980s revealed a distressing lack of understanding of the effects of sound from a neurological and/or psychological perspective. Most studies were confined to the effects of classical music on such parameters as blood pressure, respiration and heart rate. In the United States, very little had been done on the effects of sound or music on brain wave activity.

Recognizing a need for rigorous scientific study in this area, he founded Acoustic Brain Research (ABR) in 1983 to study and document the effects of sound and music on consciousness. Enrolling several university researchers and independent labs, Tom began the task of  collecting data from numerous EEG studies to see what patterns might be emerging. As a scientific picture became more apparent, Tom coined the phrase "psychoacoustics" to denote the effects of acoustic stimulation on the psyche, for not only did sound create changes in brain state, it also created definite changes in the psyches of those listening.

As a result of numerous neurological and psychological studies, as well as clinical observations, Tom developed a specific type of psychoacoustic technology which he developed over the course of a decade. Much of this technology was developed to be used by therapists in the task of psychological transformation.

In addition, Tom developed a series of tapes and CDs that can be used by individuals in the privacy of their own homes. These psychoacoustic recordings cover a wide range of interests such as stress management, psychoneuroimmunology (self-healing), increased creativity and intelligence, emotional well–being, meditation and sports performance.

Much of the focus of Tom's work continues to be on the use of sound to access the more creative aspects of consciousness. It is his strong belief that we all have abilities and talents, innate genius, waiting to be tapped. Research has borne out his theory that sound can be used as a vehicle to access these more creative aspects of the body/mind.

And he has committed much of his career to the continual research and education of the public in regard to these possibilities.

INFORMATION ABOUT TOM KENYON RECORDINGS:

If you would like free information about Tom's ABR Psychoacoustic recordings, you can visit his website at *www.tomkenyon.com* or write for a free brochure to:
Tom Kenyon, PO Box 98, Orcas, WA 98280
Tel: 360/376-5781 or email *office@tomkenyon.com*.

The website offers the most information about Tom's work and includes a section on ABR's scientific research where you can view EEG recordings and read some of the research abstracts. *Note:* If you don't have a computer, most public libraries do and can assist you.

OTHER TAPES, CDS, AND BOOKS BY TOM KENYON
Psychoacoustic Tapes from Acoustic Brain Research
The following are available through Tom Kenyon, P.O. Box 98, Orcas, WA 98280.
See website *www.tomkenyon.com* or email *office@tomkenyon.com*

RELAXATION AND STRESS MANAGEMENT
Wave Form
Gently massages your brain, dissolving tensions by creating deeply relaxing states of awareness. Theta (7HZ) Cassette $13.95, CD $16.95

Wave Form 2
Designed to open the heart. Beautiful vocals intertwined with deep harmonic musical passages. Theta (7HZ) Cassette $13.95, CD $16.95

Rest and Relaxation (R & R)
Includes 22 minute nap and 22 minute vacation. Rest for busy people who don't have time. Low Delta to Mid-Alpha (0.5-10 HZ) Cassette $13.95

Homage to Sol
Based on Lozanov Institute discoveries. Beautiful tempos for guitar, flute and cello. Relaxing and soothing. Perfect for accelerated learning. Cassette $13.95

INCREASED MIND/BRAIN PERFORMANCE
Creative Imaging
A unique combination of relaxing music and natural ambient sounds. Comes with instructions on how to significantly improve analytical abilities, creative problem solving, learning and insight. Mid-Alpha (8-10HZ) Cassette $13.95

Mind Gymnastics
ABR's flagship—hailed by researchers, professionals and lay persons as a highly innovative and powerful tool for helping to increase mental abilities and performance. Users report expanded creativity, speed of processing, and perceptual clarity. Lowest Delta to K-Complex (0.5-33HZ) 6 tapes $99.95

The Zone
For use during aerobic exercises. Increases self-motivation and encourages more intense workout. Alpha (10HZ) Cassette $13.95

SELF-HEALING AND RECOVERY
Psycho-immunology
Widely acclaimed "self-healing" program explores body/mind connection. Designed to assist in natural self-healing. Not a substitute for medical treatment. Delta, Theta, Alpha (2HZ-10HZ) 3 cassettes $49.95

Yoga for the Eyes
Eye movement exercises, guided imagery and musical patterms to help rejuvenate strained and stress weary sight. Alpha (10HZ) Cassette $13.95

Freedom To Be
Designed as a recovery assist program for alcoholism and drug addiction, also very helpful for issues of low self-esteem, self-sabotage, and emotional overwhelm. Theta (7HZ) Two cassettes $29.95

Tranformation Now!
Highly intense psychoacoustic stimulation of the brain/mind for rapid personal transformation. Rapid shifts between Alpha, Theta and High Delta (4 HZ-22HZ) (not recommended for epileptics and persons with brain damage without professional supervision) Cassette $13.95

Healing the Child Within
Unique guided imagery helps resolve deeply held childhood issues. Theta to Alpha (7-10HZ) Cassette $13.95

MEDITATION
The Ghandarva Experience
Powerful journey into spiritual realms of being. Tom created this Ghandarva Ceremony to contact the Ghandarvic Realms and sing praises to the Sacred. In this he explains the Ghandarva, then sings the Chant of the Archangels, the Calling of the Sacred Names and a beautiful rendition of the 23rd Psalm. This CD has gone around the world and is dedicated to the ecumenical spirit in all religions. Cassette $13.95, CD $16.95

Singing Crystal Bowls
Ethereal sounds of quartz "singing crystal bowls" to enhance altered states of awareness. Cassette $13.95

OTHER BOOKS BY TOM KENYON
Brain States
Must reading for anyone interested in their limitless potential. Clear and brilliant understanding of the brain. Paperback, 287 pages $11.95

The Hathor Material
Messages From An Ascended Civilization
Co-authored by Tom Kenyon and Virginia Essene, this compelling book offers highly beneficial information for the acceleration of personal evolution as offered by a group of Interdimensional beings known as the Hathors. Paperback, 226 pages. $12.95

Hathors Self-Master Exercises
Tape goes with Hathor Material and guides you through the Hathor exercises. Cassette $9.95

TOM KENYON'S LATEST RELEASES
The following are available through Tom Kenyon, P.O. Box 98, Orcas, WA 98280.
See website *www.tomkenyon.com* or email *office@tomkenyon.com*

---

*"His music and his heart are the closest
to God that I have ever felt."*
—Ken Page

City of Hymns
A unique sound healing treatment of well-known traditional hymns. Unlike anything you have ever heard before, Tom has captured the sometimes hidden healing essence in these songs. One reviewer has called Tom's voice quite simply, "the Voice of God." To hear this beautiful recording is to be transported into the spiritual and celestial realms of healing. $16.95 CD, Cassette $13.95

"Exquisitely beautiful interpretations of traditional Christian hymns delivered in a Sound Healing Treatment by Tom Kenyon, one of the most respected sound healers in the world today. This is amazing grace!"

Forbidden Songs
Tom's extraordinary songs of passion, desperation and enlightenment. These beautiful original songs will stun you with their deep and intimate sharing. This is the kind of CD that you will carry with you and play, over and over, day after day, year after year. $16.95 CD, Cassette $13.95

Tom's original songs and music. Your heart will crack, burst and rekindle to Tom's original songs of passion, desperation and enlightenment. You will tremble at this voice.

Sound Transformations
This remarkable and rare recording consists of digitally recorded toning sessions from various workshops. For years people have requested a CD of Tom's sound healing sessions which are powerfully transformative. Using his nearly four octave range voice, Tom also uses a variety of indigenous and sacred instruments to create profound alterations in consciousness. To hear this recording is to be deeply touched. Hearing is believing. $16.95 CD, Cassette $13.95

These are pistine digital "lifts" of Tom Kenyon's almost four octave voice toning live in workshops. Unbelievable! Profoundly consciousness-altering. For years people have asked for a CD with Tom toning on it. Previously, the only way to experience this was in-person at a workshop.

Tools for Inner Exploration
These are tools and meditations originally created specifically for use in workshops and are now being made available for general use. Please check our website for new offerings of these tools designed for exploring inner consciousness.

WORKSHOPS, TRAININGS, AND SACRED TOURS

Tom regularly conducts seminars in the United States and Europe. These cover a wide range of topics, reflecting his interests in many areas of human potential.

Many of these workshops are open to the general public and are designed for the layperson interested in rapid personal transformation. Due to the intensive nature of Tom's sound work which uses his nearly four octave range voice, only those desiring authentic and powerful changes should consider studying with him.

In addition, some of these trainings are specifically geared for professionals and require a background in mental health and/or medicine.

Occasionally Tom conducts tours to sacred places to be immersed in the culture that birthed a particular practice or spiritual tradition. On these tours, intensive inner work is part of the experience.

If you would like to be put on our mailing list to receive yearly schedules and occasional updates, you can email **office@tomkenyon.com** or write: **Tom Kenyon, PO Box 98, Orcas, WA 98280**. Our schedule of events is also regularly posted on his website **www.tomkenyon.com**.